Pond Perfection for Beginners

Create and Enjoy a Thriving Garden Pond

Mark Wilson

POND PERFECTION FOR BEGINNERS
Create and Enjoy a Thriving Garden Pond
© 2025 Mark Wilson

All rights reserved. No part of this book may be copied, reproduced, stored in a retrieval system, or transmitted in any form or by any means—electronic, mechanical, photocopying, recording, scanning, or otherwise—without prior written permission from the publisher, except for brief quotations used in reviews or articles.

ISBN: 9781068385605 Paperback

Published by: Inspired By Publishing

The strategies and insights in this book are provided for educational and informational purposes. Every effort has been made to trace copyright holders and obtain permission for any third-party materials used.

The information shared is based on the author's extensive personal experience with garden water features. However, results may vary, and no guarantees are made regarding specific outcomes. As with any project or activity, there are inherent risks, and the author assumes no liability for any actions taken based on the contents of this book.

The author reserves the right to make changes to this material and assumes no responsibility or liability for how it is used by readers or purchasers.

For additional resources, step-by-step guides, and companion services to support your pond-building journey, visit:

https://waterfeature.shop/pond-perfection-for-beginners

Contents

Starting with a Droplet 1

Chapter 1 - The Joys And Benefits Of Owning A Pond 13

Chapter 2 - Choosing The Perfect Spot For Your Pond 31

Chapter 3 - Types Of Ponds For Beginners 51

Chapter 4 - Planning And Designing Your Pond 71

Chapter 5 - Step-By-Step Pond Installations 91

Chapter 6 - Tips For Selecting Pond Plants
and Aquatic Life 133

Chapter 7 - Keeping It Beautiful With Minimal Effort ... 153

Chapter 8 - Troubleshooting Common
Pond Problems 171

Chapter 9 - The Pond as a Family Project 191

Chapter 10 - Embracing the Pond Lifestyle 203

Conclusion 219

Starting with a Droplet

What if I told you that a single shovel of soil could transform your garden and your connection to nature – and even yourself?

Imagine an 11-year-old boy, hands gripping a worn shovel and heart pounding with excitement as he digs his first pond in the corner of his mum's garden. That boy was me. The pond I created was far from perfect – too close to a tree, poorly planned – but it sparked something extraordinary: a lifelong passion for natural water features that bring tranquillity, nature and life into gardens.

I saved every penny from my six paper rounds to fund my pond obsession. It wasn't easy, and I made plenty of mistakes – like when I "borrowed" fish from a neighbour's pond, only to tragically lose the biggest one in my crude setup. Those early experiences taught me invaluable lessons about preparation, responsibility and care. My fish thrived because of what I got right, and when they didn't, I learned the importance of patience and adaptability.

That first pond in 1989 wasn't just a garden feature; it started a journey that shaped my life and career. That modest project under a sprawling plum tree revealed the beauty and complexity of creating an ecosystem.

A Ripple That Grew

Over the years, my passion has taken me further than I ever imagined. I've built hundreds of ponds, taught millions of enthusiasts through my YouTube channel and workshops at Pond College and witnessed how ponds can transform not just gardens but lives. Each project, from small bubbling water features to intricate koi ponds, has taught me something new about balance, beauty and the art of creating a thriving ecosystem.

But one thing stood out – there was no comprehensive, beginner-friendly guide to help people confidently start their pond journey. Too many pond owners dive into the deep end without the right tools, insights or planning, leading to frustration and avoidable mistakes. I wrote this book to fill that gap. Whether you dream of a tranquil fish pond, a haven for wildlife or a simple water feature that brings life to your patio, this book will guide you through every step. You'll find practical advice, inspiration and solutions to create a pond you'll be proud of – without the headaches of trial and error.

Building a pond is more than just a project; it's a journey of discovery, creativity and transformation. I could never have imagined its ripple effects on my life. Armed with a shovel and a pocketful of dreams, I began creating a watery sanctuary in my mum's garden. That first step set the stage for a lifelong connection with nature, water and the art of pond building.

Born From Experience

I have many reflections from my pond journey, which turned an obsession into a profession, a hobby into a lifestyle and mistakes into wisdom.

These reflections result from countless hours spent digging, experimenting and learning, fuelled by the determination to help you. Together, we'll create aquatic art that transforms gardens and inspires nature.

One of my YouTube video viewers, Sarah, sent me an email that still resonates:

"Your advice is first class and gave me the confidence to start on my own. Now, my garden pond is the highlight of our family garden."

That's why I wrote this book. I want to give you the tools, knowledge and confidence to create a pond that thrives with minimal effort and reflects your unique style and vision.

Passing on the Ripple

Every pond I've built has taught me something new. From grand koi palaces to humble wildlife havens, each project has its own challenges and rewards. And what is the biggest lesson I've learned along the way? Perfection doesn't exist – and that's okay. Your pond doesn't need to be flawless to be beautiful. What truly matters is that it reflects your creativity, effort and passion. The unique touches you bring, the lessons you learn through the process and the joy you experience watching it thrive – that's what makes a pond special.

When I built my first pond, I didn't have the tools, resources or knowledge I needed. But I had two things that mattered most: curiosity and determination. That's all you need to start. This resource is designed to offer you everything you need: the guidance, insights and encouragement to turn your vision into a reality, whether you dream of a tranquil oasis for fish, a thriving haven for wildlife or a simple water feature that brings life to your garden.

As your pond advisor, guide and mentor, I'm here to pass on the ripple – to help you avoid common mistakes, make confident decisions and enjoy the journey of pond creation. It's not just about digging a hole and filling it with water; it's about creating something meaningful and lasting.

The Beginner Advantage

Here's why striving to remain a beginner is not only valuable but essential. In the world of garden ponds, the beginner's mindset is a treasure that often gets lost as we gain experience. However, staying a beginner – or at least embracing one's curiosity, excitement and openness – can make all the difference in one's journey.

Celebrate the beginner mindset as a strength. Beginners ask questions, think creatively and are open to learning – qualities that lead to better results.

One of the most valuable lessons I've learned over the years is the importance of approaching every project as a beginner and being open to improvements. Yes, I trust myself, but even after decades of pond building, I still ask questions, experiment boldly and stay open to new ideas. Being a beginner isn't a limitation; it's a strength. Beginners ask questions that seasoned builders might overlook. They see opportunities for creativity and innovation where others see routine. Staying curious allows you to push boundaries, try new approaches and create a pond that's uniquely yours.

I will be your companion in that process. I'm here to answer your questions, spark your creativity and provide the knowledge you need to succeed. Whether starting with a small bubbling feature or dreaming of a new fish pond, this resource will help you build a foundation for a pond you love.

Your Path to a Garden Pond

Reflecting on Your Pond Dreams

As you turn these pages, I encourage you to pause and reflect on your pond dreams. What do you imagine your pond will bring to your garden? Is it:

A peaceful spot to enjoy your morning coffee?

A haven for frogs, dragonflies and birds?

A stunning feature that amazes your guests?

Take a moment to jot down your thoughts. I aim to be the spark that transforms your vision into reality.

Ask yourself:

- What kind of pond will bring me the most joy?
  - Does it matter if we have fish?
  - Does it matter if we have the sound of moving water?
- How will I balance beauty, functionality and ease of maintenance?
- What unique features – like waterfalls, lilies or pebble beaches – can make my pond truly mine?

You're taking the first step on your pond-building journey by engaging with these questions.

Charting Your Path

Everyone approaches pond building differently. Some dive straight in, shovel in hand, ready to create something extraordinary. Others prefer to pause, plan meticulously, and ensure every detail is perfect before starting. Both approaches can work, but preparation always pays off.

Here are some paths you might consider:

- **Online research.** A vast resource, but often a maze of conflicting advice.
- **Hands-on events**. Workshops like those at Pond College can fast-track your knowledge.
- **Trial and error**. Effective but often time-consuming, costly and frustrating.

By following the guidance in this book (a shortcut to success, condensing decades of experience into practical, actionable steps), you'll save time, avoid common mistakes and achieve professional results without frustration from trial and error.

Avoiding Costly Mistakes

Many beginners eagerly start digging but lack a clear plan or the proper equipment. While their intentions are good, the results often fall short, leading to:

- **Poor water quality**: Algae blooms and struggling fish are common.
- **Leaky liners**: Inadequate materials often fail over time.
- **Overcomplicated setups**: These become a maintenance nightmare with many headaches.
- **Unbalanced ecosystems**: These ponds must attract wildlife and support plants, not repel them.

I know these pitfalls because I've been there. By starting with the right foundation – planning, proper materials, and proven techniques – you'll avoid headaches and create a pond that's a source of pride, not a burden.

How We'll Get You There

This isn't just a "how-to" manual; it's a companion on your journey. It is tailored for total beginners and combines decades of hands-on experience, practical advice and insights to fast-track your journey to success.

From planning to troubleshooting, here's how I will easily walk you through every stage of your pond-building journey:

- **Planning.** Choosing the right pond type, size and location for your lifestyle and garden.
- **Building.** Step-by-step instructions, from excavation to installing liners and filtration systems.
- **Planting.** Selecting and arranging aquatic plants for beauty, balance and ease of care.

- **Maintaining.** Keeping your pond clean, thriving and low-maintenance.
- **Troubleshooting.** Solving common issues like algae blooms or equipment problems.
- **Step-by-Step Guidance.** Each chapter offers clear, actionable steps from planning and building to planting and maintaining.
- **Mistakes to Avoid.** Learn and take notes from my past mistakes to save you time and effort in the long run.
- **Creative Inspiration.** Discover how to make your pond reflect your style and personality.
- **Reflecting.** Embracing the journey of creating something meaningful while learning and growing.

Throughout the book, you'll find checklists, bullet points and quick tips to make each chapter actionable and easy to revisit. Whether you're a novice or have dabbled in pond building, this resource saves you time, money and heartache by offering a clear path to success.

Why Start Now?

There's never been a better time to begin your pond journey. Here's why:

- **Reconnect with nature.** Transform your garden into a haven of tranquillity where birds, dragonflies and other wildlife come to life around your pond.
- **Make an environmental impact.** Your pond supports local ecosystems, offering a sanctuary for

frogs, insects and other creatures while promoting biodiversity.

- **Save money, achieve more.** Rising professional service costs make DIY pond building both budget-friendly and deeply rewarding. With my encouraging words, you can create a stunning pond at a fraction of the cost.
- **Turn "someday" into "today."** How often do we delay our dreams, thinking we'll start "someday"? Let this book help you take that first step, transforming hesitation into years of joy and fulfilment.
- **Grow personally.** Building a pond isn't just about the result – it's about the journey. You'll gain new skills, solve creative challenges and experience the pride of bringing your vision to life.

A Journey Worth Taking

Building your first pond is like planting a seed. It starts small, but with the proper care and guidance, it grows into something extraordinary. I wish I could hand you this book while we sit beside a pond you're already proud of. But the exciting part is that the pond is within reach, and you're pages away from the first step toward making it a reality.

Let's embark on this journey together. Whether this is your first pond or your fifth, every project begins with a single step. That first shovel of earth and ripple of water is the start of something amazing. By the end of this book, you'll have the tools, confidence and inspiration to create a pond that reflects your vision, care and creativity.

Your pond will be more than a feature in your garden – it will be a living testament to your effort and passion, a source of pride, serenity and joy. Together, we'll transform your dream into reality, creating a space that nurtures life and beauty. Every ripple makes an impact.

Beginners Build with Purpose

A beginner's pond is always built with intention – whether to create a sanctuary for wildlife, a tranquil retreat for relaxation or a lively space for entertaining guests. Staying a beginner means regularly revisiting the purpose behind your pond and ensuring it continues to align with your goals and lifestyle.

Ask yourself, is this my pond? Is my pond bringing joy, or has it become a source of stress? Does it still reflect the vision I had when I first started?

When reading each chapter, remember:

Perfection doesn't exist. And that's a good thing. Your pond will evolve, just like you. Embrace the imperfections – they're part of the beauty.

Start small, dream big. You don't need a grand design or endless resources to create something extraordinary.

Start with what you have, and let your passion grow from there.

The right pond shouldn't rule your life. A well-designed pond is a source of joy, not a burden. With the proper planning, you can leave it in good hands while you go on holiday, knowing your fish and plants will thrive.

Every ripple starts with a single drop. Whether you're digging your first pond or your tenth, every project begins with the courage to start. That first ripple can transform your garden, mindset and life.

Close your eyes and imagine the sound of trickling water, the sight of dragonflies darting above a shimmering pond, and the peace it brings to your garden. Building a pond isn't just about creating a feature – it's about transforming your space and reconnecting with nature.

So, let's dig that first hole, place that first stone and create a pond that reflects your vision and care. As you read this book, you'll gain the tools, knowledge and confidence to make your pond dream a reality. Let's begin the journey – one ripple at a time.

Want more guidance or questions to ask yourself? Explore our in-depth **Pond Planning Checklist.** Visit https://waterfeature.shop/planning-checklist for a detailed guide and expert insights.

Chapter 1
THE JOYS AND BENEFITS OF OWNING A POND

Before we start digging, let's start with "Why?"

This chapter is essential because it sets the foundation for why you should consider building a pond in the first place. It doesn't matter whether you pick up the tools or hire someone to create the pond for you. In this chapter, I want to highlight the joys and benefits of ponds and share how some of my clients have connected emotionally with their ponds. Finding your "why" means you can start with the proper foundation or even add to the ideas you currently have about owning a garden pond. I want you to start seeing it as more than just a decorative feature – instead, think of it as a valuable addition to your lifestyle.

You'll learn about the various ways a pond can change your garden and your life while benefiting the environment by supporting local wildlife.

Let's begin with you, a nature lover and someone who understands the joys of the outdoors. You want to bring a little piece of nature closer to home so you can enjoy the outdoors more often. In this first chapter, I focus on the emotional fulfilment and the environmental impact of a new pond, how it introduces tranquillity and the personal benefits of owning a pond.

Most beginners are worried about taking the first step, and I encourage everyone to start small and focus on creating a pond that meets their needs, whether it's a wildlife pond or a decorative garden feature. Some people follow this advice about starting small, and others like the challenge of biting off more than they can chew or hiring a professional with years of experience. As you will soon see, you don't need to be overwhelmed by the technical aspects – unless you want something much more complex than what's outlined in Chapter 5 or even more advanced features. Just remember, when doing the work, it's about the joy of creating something unique in your garden that can be built on over time.

A Personal Sanctuary

The Health Benefits of Ponds

A pond is more than just a beautiful garden feature; it's a space that nurtures your emotional well-being and offers real health benefits. By incorporating water into your garden, you create a sanctuary that invites you to slow down, breathe deeply and enjoy moments of peace.

Start with a Vision

Think about what you want to achieve through a garden pond. It is best to complete the statement, "I'm happy when…"

Will it be a peaceful retreat? (*I'm happy when* I have no distractions).

Will it be a space for wildlife? (*I'm happy when* I have created a better space for local wildlife).

Will it be a place for entertainment? (*I'm happy when* we all get together).

A pond can provide all of these things. You just need to think about what matters the most to you and your family: a calming retreat to relieve stress, a meditative space for mindfulness and a place where nature can flourish and more.

Ponds bring a unique blend of beauty and tranquillity to any garden, transforming even the most unadorned spaces into personal sanctuaries. The combination of water, lush plants and the gentle sounds of nature creates a peaceful environment that helps you unwind and escape the stresses of everyday life.

The rippling water, surrounded by greenery or illuminated with subtle lighting, elevates your garden into a tranquil retreat. A pond can become the focal point of your outdoor space, offering a place to reflect, relax and reconnect with nature. Whether enjoying the stillness at the end of the day or simply taking in the view, a well-designed pond enriches your landscape and well-being.

Cold Water Immersion

For those interested in cold-water immersion, ponds offer a natural space to incorporate this practice into their routine. You don't need a large swim pond – even just dipping your feet in the water can release endorphins, boosting your mood and energy levels. Over time, this practice helps train the nervous system to handle stress more effectively, strengthening mental and physical resilience.

In addition to the physical benefits, cold water immersion encourages mental fortitude. Willingly stepping into or sitting in cold water requires overcoming discomfort, which can help sharpen focus, improve alertness and better equip you to manage stress throughout the day.

Mindfulness and Relaxation

A pond provides a calming space for relaxation, mindfulness and stress reduction. The presence of water creates an atmosphere of tranquillity, encouraging you to slow down and focus on the peaceful surroundings. Whether it's the sound of a waterfall or the gentle ripples on the surface, the soothing effect of water helps calm a busy mind and foster moments of reflection.

A pond becomes a natural retreat where you can disconnect from the pressures of daily life and immerse yourself in nature. Quiet activities like observing wildlife or tending to aquatic plants enhance well-being and mindfulness. Time spent near a garden pond offers therapeutic benefits, lowering cortisol levels and reducing anxiety.

A pond is more than a garden feature – it becomes a personal sanctuary for restoring mental and emotional balance. Take a moment to stop, pause and visualise your ideal pond space. Picture how you would use it and jot down your thoughts.

The Role Ponds Play in Supporting Biodiversity

A well-maintained garden pond can help combat climate change. Although you might think one small garden pond will not help, all garden ponds absorb carbon and create natural habitats that offset urbanisation.

Ponds enhance local biodiversity, attracting wildlife and supporting the ecosystem. They also help conserve water, as ponds can collect rainwater that might otherwise go to waste. Natural ponds can even become self-sustaining ecosystems, helping your garden thrive and contributing to a healthier local environment.

Ponds are vital in enhancing local biodiversity by creating thriving habitats for various wildlife. From birds and frogs to insects and aquatic creatures, a pond naturally attracts species that rely on water for survival, nesting and reproduction. By providing a consistent water source, ponds become an essential oasis for local wildlife, helping to sustain populations and promote ecological balance.

Nature ponds, or still-water wildlife ponds, are designed to mimic natural water bodies. They support visible wildlife and microorganisms that contribute to a healthy ecosystem. These ponds encourage biodiversity by offering different zones for various species, such as shallow edges for amphibians and deeper sections for fish. Adding native plants around the pond's perimeter further enhances its role as a wildlife haven, providing food and shelter for birds, bees and butterflies.

Garden ponds also conserve water by capturing rainwater that lands directly or is directed from buildings via pipes. In fact, most garden ponds I saw in the '90s collected rainwater for the vegetables growing in the gardens. Aquatic plants can naturally filter rainwater or even grey water (as reed bed filtration is becoming more popular), keeping the pond clean while improving the surroundings and any water that overflows. This natural filtration and water management system supports a balanced, self-sustaining ecosystem that contributes to local environmental health. Whether in a small garden or a larger landscape, a pond can significantly improve the biodiversity and ecological richness of the area, making it an essential feature for nature lovers and conservationists alike.

Many clients have discovered these benefits firsthand: I would like to share their stories with you.

How a Pond Became a Haven for Birds and Frogs

A newly retired couple approached us with the desire to transform their garden into a more peaceful, nature-filled space. They wanted a pond but needed to figure out how they would interact with it. When they hired us, they envisioned a simple water feature to enhance their garden's aesthetic. Little did they know how much the pond would come to mean to them.

After we installed the pond, something unexpected happened – what started as a beautiful addition to their garden quickly became a wildlife haven, especially for birds and frogs. The husband, who had never taken much interest in birdwatching before, was captivated by the variety of birds visiting the pond. The pond drew in more species than they could have imagined, from robins and blackbirds to the odd kingfisher. He soon invested in a pair of binoculars and a DSLR camera, spending his early mornings observing the birds quietly and photographing them as they drank from the pond and bathed in the shallow areas.

On the other hand, his wife rediscovered her childhood love for frogs. As a young girl, she had always been fascinated by them, and now, with their new pond, she found herself delighted by their regular appearances. We added willow moss to help shelter tadpoles and provide a place in the early spring for frogs to spawn. During one of my service calls, I recommended some floating islands to help the little froglets escape and not become lunch for the birds. Around the pond, we added some small hostas that attract slugs so the frogs could enjoy eating them instead of using pellets. In spring, the couple watched in awe as the pond became a breeding ground for frogs, with tadpoles swimming freely among the aquatic plants. The wife even went as far as creating small hideaways and planting specific foliage to encourage more frogs to make their home in the garden.

A simple desire to enhance their garden evolved into a shared passion for wildlife. The pond brought them closer to nature, filling their retirement with new hobbies: birdwatching and frog conservation. For this couple, the pond became more than just a garden feature; it became a focal point for enjoying life's simple pleasures and deepening their connection with the natural world.

Transforming a Neglected Garden into a Thriving Ecosystem

A client came to me with a neglected garden that needed serious attention. Their back garden was overrun with ivy. After reading inspirational books and watching my YouTube videos about safely building a wildlife pond with moving water, they decided to take the plunge and create a small waterfall and pond to turn their space into a nature-friendly haven.

Despite not being highly skilled at DIY, my client was determined to build a pond that would attract wildlife and add beauty to their garden. They even went as far as planning a "bug hotel" and planting a selection of shrubs and reeds to encourage further biodiversity. They created a "beach" area in their pond to allow easy access for local hedgehogs and other wildlife. We worked together early on to figure out the best placement for the wildlife pond filtration, which included an intake bay (an area next to the pond where the pond pump is located, which is much more wildlife-friendly) and a waterfall filter (designed to create a beautiful water feature).

What started as a blank canvas of overgrown borders and ivy has now blossomed into a thriving ecosystem that looks beautiful and supports local wildlife – proof that even a neglected garden corner can become a natural retreat with the right vision and guidance.

How Feeding Fish Became a Daily Ritual for a Busy Executive

I have a client who is a high-performing executive in a fast-paced industry. He initially sought a pond to create a sense of calm in his garden. He imagined it would be a peaceful retreat from the demands of his work, a place to decompress. However, he didn't foresee how deeply connected he would become to feeding his fish. It soon became an unexpected highlight in his daily routine.

Once the pond was installed and stocked with koi, it quickly transformed into his sanctuary. After long days filled with meetings and deadlines, he instinctively gravitated toward the pond when he got home, saying to his family, "Just going out to feed the boys." Feeding the fish became more than a task; it became a meditative ritual, a chance to forget work. Before the pond was built, it took him much longer to transition from business to being a husband and father. The moment he sprinkled food and hand-fed treats into the water, he was met with the graceful movements of the fish swimming eagerly to the surface, which forged a sense of connection with nature entirely different from the pressures of his work life.

He shared with me how these moments offered a deep sense of grounding. The gentle splash of water, the sound of the fish when they fed and the pond's tranquil beauty let his mind release the day's stress. The simple act of observing the fish helped him feel the rhythm of nature. The fish sometimes even made him laugh! Interacting with this ecosystem became his escape, a routine that signalled his shift from the intensity of the workday to the calm of home life.

For this client, feeding the fish wasn't just about watching them swim. It soon became a form of mindfulness, a daily practice that reconnected him with the present moment and allowed him to leave work at the pond's edge. Over time, this small act evolved into a necessary form of relaxation. It became his way of transitioning from the fast pace of the office to the peace and stillness of home. As he took a few moments to engage with his pond each day, he noticed his mood lift and his stress levels decrease. Over time, he saw the return of his ability to truly enjoy his evenings.

For this executive, the pond became more than a beautiful feature; it became the centre of a daily ritual, a source of mental clarity and a retreat that offered physical and emotional rejuvenation.

Craft a Pond to Bring Your Family Together

Ponds naturally unite people, becoming a central point for creating lasting family memories. Whether families gather for outdoor picnics, to teach children about nature, or to enjoy quiet moments together, a pond provides the perfect backdrop for family connection. It's not just about owning a water feature – it's about buying quality time.

Many pond builders understand this well. When professionals design and install ponds, they aren't just selling a decorative feature; they're offering a way for families to bond. I often hear stories of children interacting with the pond, watching tadpoles grow and learning about ecosystems first-hand. These moments of discovery and connection foster a deeper appreciation for nature while creating memories that last a lifetime.

As a child, I loved collecting clumps of frog spawn from friends' ponds and watching them grow in aquariums, though I now know it's better to observe them in their natural habitat. I love showing children how to interact responsibly with wildlife, whether watching tadpoles grow legs or seeing how much they love a simple treat like processed chicken. These small, hands-on experiences teach kids about the natural world in a fun and engaging way.

The calming presence of water also has a unique effect, similar to sitting by a campfire. Families often find that spending time near a pond helps them relax, unwind and focus on the moment. Whether gathered around the pond on a summer evening or simply sitting by the water with a cup of tea, a pond creates a serene atmosphere that fosters conversation and connection.

Again, a pond is more than a water feature. It becomes the heart of your garden, where family memories are made and nature's quiet beauty draws everyone together.

An Experiment in Transforming Atmosphere

My wife Charlotte was reading her book, and I was on my phone one afternoon when a thought suddenly came to mind: What would happen if I turned off the standalone waterfall and stream next to where we were sitting? I mentioned it to Charlotte so she wouldn't think we had lost power, and with a remote control in hand, I switched off the water feature.

Within seconds, the atmosphere completely changed. Suddenly, the sounds we hadn't even noticed before became clear – people talking, lawnmowers running, children playing in the park, distant traffic and even a siren on the dual carriageway.

The calm we had been enjoying seemed to vanish, replaced by the hustle and bustle of everyday life.

After a few minutes, Charlotte looked up from her book and suggested going inside. But I said, "Wait a second," and turned the water feature back on. Instantly, the world around us quieted. The sounds of the outside world faded into the background and were replaced by the gentle flow of water, creating a cocoon of tranquillity. We both laughed, amazed at how quickly the calming effect returned. We had been sitting there for hours without realising it, enjoying the peaceful ambience the water feature provided.

This small experiment was a big "Aha!" moment for both of us. It demonstrated how much a water feature can transform the atmosphere of a garden. In a noisy environment, the sound of water drowns out distractions, creating a peaceful retreat where you can relax and feel miles away from the busyness around you.

The experience also reminded us of how nature subtly interacts with this tranquil space. As we sat, a pigeon dropped down from our big holly tree, drank quickly from the feature and flew off again. We looked at each other and smiled – it was a small but powerful reminder of the simple joys that a pond can bring to your garden.

Whether you live in a quiet rural area or a bustling urban environment, a water feature can serve as a sound buffer, turning even the noisiest garden into a serene retreat. It becomes the heartbeat of your outdoor space, transforming your garden's overall mood and atmosphere.

Transform Your Garden, Transform Your Life

A busy couple with demanding jobs and a hectic family life wanted a way to create memorable moments of peace and connection at home. They envisioned their garden as a space to unwind and spend quality time together without travelling. After discussing various ideas during a design consultation, we installed a beautifully illuminated pond with subtle underwater lighting and a fire pit feature.

When the project was finished, their garden became a haven of tranquillity, especially in the evenings. The couple quickly established a new ritual: Once the day's chaos had settled, they would make hot chocolate or mulled wine and retreat to their garden. Sitting next to the glowing pond, surrounded by the soft lights reflecting off the water and warmed by the naked flames of their firepit, they found a serene space to reconnect.

They shared how this time had become their "escape" – a place to talk, laugh and enjoy each other's company without distractions. The orange glow of the fire, the illuminated pond and the calming sound of water made their garden feel like a luxurious retreat.

The ritual became especially cherished in the colder months as they wrapped themselves up, watched the gentle steam rise from their mugs and felt the warmth of the flames.

For this couple, their pond became an intimate space for quality time, transforming ordinary moments into cherished memories. Their evenings by the pond became a regular tradition, reminding them to slow down and savour life's simple pleasures amid the rush of daily responsibilities.

Overcoming Fears to Build a Wildlife Pond

One client reached out to me after finally deciding to take the plunge and create a wildlife pond themselves, something they had been hesitant to do for years. Their hesitation stemmed from a few common fears that often hold people back from starting such a project. They were primarily worried about maintenance, wondering if the pond would become a burden over time. They had heard stories of ponds that turned murky, overrun with algae or became too difficult to manage, leaving them concerned about the time and effort required to keep the pond healthy and beautiful.

Another concern was the appearance. The client feared investing time, money and energy only to end up with something that didn't match their vision or became an eyesore in their garden. The idea of creating a pond from scratch felt daunting, especially without much prior DIY experience. These doubts delayed their project for years as they debated whether a pond was the right decision.

With a bit of guidance and some inspiration from my YouTube videos, they finally embarked on their pond-building journey and were amazed at the results:

> *"I never thought I'd have a pond because I was always too afraid to start and worried about what the end product would look like. But now that it's done, my pond is crystal clear, and I can't believe how well it turned out! It's just waiting for the plants to establish and the wildlife to arrive."*

While their excitement grew as the project took shape, some concerns still lingered, particularly about water clarity:

> *"The only thing I'm worried about now is, can it be too clear? I'm afraid now, Mark, that the filtration system*

> *might be stripping too much algae from the water and leaving insufficient food for wildlife."*

This story highlights the typical journey from fear to fulfilment when creating a pond. Initial doubts and fears about maintenance and aesthetics are common but can be overcome with the correct planning, tools and guidance. With the proper plant choices and ongoing care, their pond quickly became a haven for wildlife, demonstrating the deep sense of accomplishment and connection with nature that comes from building a pond.

If you're facing similar fears, take heart.

Proper planning and the right choices can turn these common fears into rewarding challenges. Start by seeking inspiration online. Watch our showcases and transformation videos:
https://waterfeature.shop/showcases

Then, ask to visit other people's ponds similar to the one you want to create. It is best to find nature lovers who've made these ponds themselves (reach out to friends or visit our gardens). Doing preliminary research will help you find practical tips and gain confidence in creating a thriving ecosystem in your garden.

A pond can turn any garden into a peaceful retreat. The sight and sound of water, lush plants and fish create a relaxing atmosphere that soothes the mind. Whether sitting by the pond with a cup of tea or listening to the gentle ripple of water after a long day, the sense of peace brought about by a water feature is undeniable.

Building and maintaining a pond also gives one a sense of pride and ownership. Watching your pond grow, seeing wildlife thrive and knowing you created this natural sanctuary is incredibly fulfilling. It's about the result and the journey of learning, building and enjoying your pond.

Owning a pond is more than just having a water feature. It's an opportunity to create a personal oasis that brings joy, supports the environment and enhances your lifestyle.

If you plan to build your first pond, I encourage you to start small. Picture your ideal pond and embark on this journey with me. We can break it down into phases. Whether your goal is to attract wildlife, create a peaceful retreat or establish a gathering place for family and friends, the possibilities are endless.

Chapter 2
CHOOSING THE PERFECT SPOT FOR YOUR POND

Choosing the perfect location for your pond is essential to creating a stunning water feature that enhances the beauty of your garden and nurtures a thriving ecosystem. This decision marks the first practical and actionable step in bringing your aquatic vision to life.

In this chapter, you'll discover how visibility, sunlight and accessibility are crucial to maximising your pond's enjoyment and sustainability. By selecting the ideal spot, you can create a pond that harmonises with your life, supports vibrant plant and aquatic life, reduces maintenance efforts and offers year-round beauty from every perspective. This choice is a vital step toward transforming your garden into a cherished sanctuary you'll love and enjoy effortlessly. Let's dive into my top tips about pond locations.

Visibility and Creating a Focal Point

Visibility is vital when choosing the location for your garden pond. Many people make the mistake of placing their pond at the far end of the garden to create a retreat or a place to go, only to find they rarely visit or enjoy it that often. Instead, I always recommend bringing your pond closer to your home. I did this with a couple that loved dragonflies. They had a sizeable leaking pond at the bottom of the garden, and they just wanted me to replace the liner. This pond was about 80 metres down a gentle slope. They didn't like the idea of moving the pond as it had always been there, and they wanted to keep the view of the whole garden from the house, so I said we could plant the pond differently in a way that does not block their view.

They often thank me for being persistent about the pond's location, and I will never forget their faces on my first return to check up on it about a month later. They both shared stories about enjoying the pond from inside the house. Can you imagine being dragonfly lovers and watching them while eating at the dining table?

Every once-a-year visit, they remark about wondrous new happenings. Their conservatory became a hide, with tripoded cameras and binoculars, allowing the enjoyment of new birds they had never seen in the garden who were now coming and spending a short time by the pond. I experienced this on my fourth visit, five years later (I had skipped a year in 2021 after the lockdown in 2020), as it was time to reduce the reeds. As I approached the back garden with my equipment, I saw they had commissioned an enormous summer house with a small deck stretching over its edge. I then took the opportunity to sit on that deck for my quick cup of coffee, and a female southern hawker landed on me. It was magical, and my customer saw it all from inside the house and remarked on the moment.

Creating a water feature that you can appreciate 365 days a year is essential. I love seeing ice formations (they change in the depths of the coldest months every day), but I don't think I would see them if they were visible from the inside or if you had no other reason to walk past. How often are you likely to visit a pond in the winter?

The solution is to ensure your pond is visible from multiple vantage points. This way, you can enjoy its beauty and tranquillity regardless of the weather, whether it's too wet or hot to venture outside (during heat waves) or too cold to sit by the water. A well-placed pond will be a constant source of pleasure, inviting you to pause and appreciate nature right outside the comfort of your home.

Positioning the pond near your house turns your property into a waterfront oasis, providing a soothing view from windows and seating areas.

The Best Way to Test a Pond's Visibility

Mark out the area with a hose pipe, landscape paint, white sand or coloured string (anything you can see easily) to get a real sense of how the pond will look and feel. During this exercise, you can also look at its size and shape.

Ask yourself: Is the pond going to be in the right place? If you live in a house, get upstairs and look out the windows; the elevation will change the pond's feel. Remember to walk around your garden to visualise how the pond will look from various spots. Live with it for a while and ensure you're 100% happy.

Avoid hiding it behind large bushes or structures that obstruct the view. By positioning a pond in an area with optimal visibility, you ensure that it becomes a main focal point of your garden, drawing the eye and enhancing the overall atmosphere of your outdoor living space.

Considering Sunlight

Imagine sipping your morning coffee while watching the reflections in the water or catching glimpses of visiting wildlife as you do your daily activities.

Sunlight is crucial in determining the health and vibrancy of your pond and its inhabitants. The right balance of sun and shade can enhance the pond's aesthetic appeal, promote healthy plant growth and support fish wellbeing. For aquatic plants like water lilies, five to six hours of sunlight daily is essential for them to bloom and thrive. Sunlight also benefits fish, helping them produce vitamin D and maintain good health. However, excessive direct sunlight can cause water temperature to rise and encourage algae growth, leading to more maintenance and a less attractive pond.

Full sun in the UK is ideal for most pond plants, particularly water lilies and flowering marginals. Our sunlight isn't as intense as in hotter climates, making it difficult for some hardy plants to bloom unless grown in a conservatory or greenhouse with supplemental grow lights. In the UK, sun exposure is essential for your pond to achieve its full potential. Your water lilies will thrive in full sun, rewarding you with beautiful blooms. However, in hotter climates, excessive sunlight can pose a big problem, and you may need to erect sunshades or use other methods to moderate the heat.

When choosing your pond's location, aim for a spot with morning sun and partial afternoon shade. This placement helps prevent overheating during the hottest day while providing enough light for plant growth. Dappled light from nearby branches or a pergola can help regulate temperature without completely blocking sunlight. Avoid placing your pond in deep shade or too close to buildings that cast shadows, as this will limit the light your plants receive. I once worked on a pond positioned too close to a garage and an extension. The shade cast by these buildings in spring and summer hindered plant growth, leading to poor flowering results.

To solve this issue, we built another water garden for the same client in a sunnier area, specifically for growing water lilies and purple irises. In full sun, the plants flourished, producing stunning flowers throughout the season.

Another example that highlights the importance of sunlight is a client who wanted a pond positioned to reflect light that she could see from her home office and studio window. As an artist, she found that the gentle ripples and changing light patterns on the pond surface provided inspiration and helped boost her productivity. She mentioned feeling less motivated to work on her art when the sunlight didn't reach the pond due to cloud cover or seasonal changes. The pond's positioning became integral to her creative process, reminding her to look outside, pause and draw inspiration from the natural world. This scenario perfectly illustrates how a well-placed pond can contribute to more than just garden aesthetics; it can enhance your daily life, provide a sense of calm and foster creativity.

By finding the right balance of sun and shade, you'll create a healthy, beautiful pond that you can enjoy all year round from various vantage points around your home and garden. Make sure to walk around your garden during different times of the day to observe how sunlight interacts with the space. This observation will help you determine the best spot for your pond, ensuring it remains a prominent feature you can appreciate regardless of season.

Accessibility

When planning your pond's location, consider how it will look and how accessible it will be for regular maintenance. A beautifully designed pond can quickly become a burden if it's difficult to reach or maintain. Leave enough space around the pond for tasks like skimming leaves (if you don't have a skimmer or your net doesn't reach across the surface), cleaning filters or trimming back plants. Leaving some space will ensure that maintaining your pond remains enjoyable rather than a chore.

Leave at least 50 cm around the pond to provide adequate space for picking your way around it via stepping stones, crouching down to weed while tending to the water or plants and other similar activities.

When designing extensive water features like streams or ponds with complex layouts, consider how these impact the surrounding garden. Avoid cutting off areas or creating narrow, awkward spaces that are hard to navigate with a ride-on lawnmower or other gardening tools. A well-thought-out pond design should integrate seamlessly into the rest of your garden, allowing you to move around freely. It shouldn't block garden access or create bottlenecks that make lawn care or maintenance difficult.

A Pond Suffering from a Hedge

Back in the naughties, I was asked to drain and clean a beautiful wildlife pond nestled at the edge of a property in Buckinghamshire. The garden was lovely, but the pond's proximity to a thick, overgrown hedge became a significant issue.

The pond itself was gorgeous, brimming with aquatic plants. But the pond had loads of conifer waste (brown sludge). The hedge behind it had grown wildly. The local gardeners refused to trim it because they couldn't maintain it safely without risking damage to the pond liner or collecting the waste. They were concerned their ladders might slip or puncture the pond liner beneath. The hatch inside the ever-green hedge would inevitably end up in the pond water, changing the pH of the pond. The gardeners simply left the hedge alone once the long-reach trimmers and other tools weren't effective.

The hedge was growing, and no one wanted to take responsibility for trimming it since the pond was so close to the hedge. The only option left was for pond specialists to handle the hedge maintenance ourselves. We had to meticulously cut it each year to avoid causing a mess and damaging the liner.

The process took us hours of careful work and each year, the challenge grew as the hedge became thicker and more unruly. It was an ongoing battle and a constant reminder that the location of a pond should take more than just aesthetics into account.

Hedges and ponds can be beautiful together, creating natural shelter and privacy. But, if not planned properly, they can cause a logistical nightmare for maintenance. If a hedge surrounds your pond, always ensure enough space to work around the entire perimeter.

In this case, had the hedge been appropriately cut from the start, it would have been okay (if it had been clipped a couple of times a year). This conifer didn't back bud, so we had no option but to remove the hedge. If the pond had been positioned a metre further away from the hedge, the gardeners would have been able to manage it without issues. This experience emphasised the importance of leaving enough clearance around the pond, not only for aesthetic purposes but also for practical maintenance. Sometimes, a slight adjustment in placement can save you years of hassle and frustration.

Avoid Heavy Debris Zones

Placing a pond too close to trees can lead to problems that affect the pond's appearance and ecosystem.

Certain trees, such as oak, chestnut, beech, walnut, pine and sycamore, can wreak havoc on ponds. They shed needles, nuts, sticky sap or toxic substances that harm fish and plant life. If placing your pond near trees is unavoidable, consider using cover nets (pitched leaf nets are the best) or other pond covers during peak shedding seasons to keep falling debris out of the water.

Roots are another issue to consider. Over time, tree roots can puncture pond liners, causing leaks and structural damage. Poor drainage around trees can also lead to waterlogging near the pond's base, complicating maintenance and increasing the risk of pond liner damage.

While shade can be beneficial, too much overhead canopy can lead to leaf buildup, water contamination and constant cleaning. If you want to position your pond near trees, ensure it's far enough away to prevent leaf fall and other debris from becoming a persistent nuisance. Consider moving the pond to a more open area or designing it with built-in protective measures like leaf nets. This positioning will save you time and effort, making your garden's pond a low-maintenance feature.

Walnuts and Goldfish

One of my most memorable learning experiences occurred in Oxfordshire, where I was called out one spring to transform an old, disused swimming pool into a stunning goldfish pond. The property owners had just moved in and didn't want the hassle of maintaining a swimming pool as they were downsizing and retiring. Instead, they envisioned a serene pond filled with colourful goldfish and blooming water lilies.

The initial setting seemed perfect. The unused pool, recently relined and sealed by the couple's builders (who had done a lot of work in and around the house), was in a beautiful garden surrounded by mature trees and right next to a grass tennis court. The swimming pool was situated directly beneath a tree with a preservation order. The couple had received permission to prune it for safety reasons due to the tennis court below.

While they couldn't remove the tree, it wasn't a significant issue, as once it started to regrow, it wouldn't cast much of a shadow over the pool. The shadow meant that we could grow water lilies in full sun. Due to the cost of the old equipment, they didn't want any water movement or filtration, so they did some quick research and decided to have a still-water nature pool. They even got the builders to remove the pumps, plumbing lines and all power near the pool before we were called to transform it with the goldfish and plants.

In the first year, everything seemed to go perfectly. We added more plinths to the pond to grow attractive water lilies and stocked the pool with more giant goldfish. The lilies thrived, their flowers spreading beautifully across the surface. With no filtration, it took extra effort to keep the pond clean, so the gardener had to remove leaves and tree waste every week. During our last visit in September, we noticed lots of baby brown goldfish swimming around—an excellent sign that the pond was establishing itself. We left for the winter with great satisfaction, looking forward to the following year's growth.

But when we returned the following spring, something was off. There was no sign of the fish. I initially thought they were hiding because the couple had only started revisiting the pool area. We assumed the fish were shy or the local herons had picked off a few, but we weren't too concerned.

A month later, there was still no movement in the pond. There were no flashes of orange or gold darting beneath the water lilies, which were growing well. Another month passed, and still nothing. The pond, now crystal clear but full of string algae, was devoid of fish. Alarmed, I investigated further, netting out the weed and inspecting the pool's base.

That's when we made a shocking discovery: I found several rotten walnut shells and leaves covering the bottom of the pond. The smell was overwhelming. I didn't realise the tree was a walnut – it was huge! It turns out that walnuts – especially when rotting – release toxins very harmful to fish. The leaves and nuts had fallen unnoticed and unremoved into the pond last autumn. The toxins must have built up over time, killing every single goldfish we had placed in the pond.

It was a hard lesson learned: Goldfish and walnut trees don't mix. Despite the gardener's best efforts and the perfect water lilies, we hadn't accounted for the walnut tree's toxicity. We advised the couple to refrain from restocking the pond with fish. Since then, I have always double-checked the types of trees surrounding a potential pond site and shared this story to help others avoid making the same mistake.

A Beautiful Formal Garden Design Under a Colossal Horse Chestnut

One of my early projects involved maintaining a stunning water feature, including a koi pool at the base set within a meticulously designed formal garden with many formal stone slabbed walkways. The whole feature was nestled beneath a sprawling horse chestnut tree, its dense canopy providing dappled shade to the water feature below. The garden layout was magnificent, with long, formal rills wound through carefully arranged channels covered in cobblestones on the base. Water flowed gently from the koi pool at the base of the garden, meandering through these rills and around the garden, creating a serene atmosphere.

It was a beautiful spot, but its location presented unique challenges. The garden was overshadowed by the massive horse chestnut, and leaves and sap regularly fell into the water. My monthly visits were primarily spent removing tree debris and clearing cobbles. What made the pond even more remarkable were the thriving beds of yellow irises that filled three rilled pools. These vibrant plants weren't just ornamental; they quietly played a crucial role in maintaining the pond's water quality by absorbing excess nutrients and filtering out toxins.

One summer, the homeowner decided that the irises were growing too aggressively and asked me to remove them. Initially, it was a reasonable request. However, shortly after I took out the bulk of the irises, we both learned a harsh lesson in pond ecology.

Without the irises' natural filtration capabilities, the pond's ecosystem became unbalanced. Fallen leaves, sticky sap and bird droppings accumulated in the water, creating water quality issues that had never been a problem before. The koi pond, which had always been crystal clear, started turning a murky black tea colour. That October, after a night of heavy wind and rainfall, I received an urgent call from the homeowner: "Mark, the fish are all dead. Can you come and sort out the pond?"

When I arrived, I was met with a heartbreaking sight. The pond and rills were choked with leaves that had fallen overnight. The pond pump was clogged entirely, causing oxygen levels to plummet. The leaves had collapsed the cover net over most of the pond. The koi, which had once swum so gracefully in the clear waters, had succumbed to the poor water conditions and lack of oxygen under the net.

This experience taught us a vital lesson: Never underestimate aquatic plants' role in maintaining pond health, especially under challenging conditions like those posed by a nearby giant tree. Removing the irises may have improved the formal garden's appearance, but it came at a tremendous cost to the fish. Now, I always advise homeowners to consider the benefits of natural filtration before changing their ponds.

Lesson learned: When placing a pond near large trees, always plan for leaf control and natural filtration, and only remove essential plants with an understanding of their impact on the ecosystem.

Ground conditions

Clay, Sloped or Unstable

Ground conditions are crucial for pond stability. A pond on a slope or uneven ground will experience water imbalance and potentially overflow. Choose a flat, stable location or consider landscaping adjustments to create a level base.

Low-lying areas prone to flooding or poor drainage can lead to *hippoing*, where water pressure pushes up the liner and bulges (groundwater pressure pushes uppressure pushes up the pond liner, making it look like a hippo's back). Place your pond on higher ground or install drainage solutions to avoid this. Roots, runoff and structural issues can also arise if the pond is built too close to trees or unstable soil. Taking the time to assess and prepare your pond site will ensure long-term success and fewer maintenance headaches.

Imagine you built a pond at the lowest point in your garden, which tends to collect water after heavy rains.

A few days later, you notice the pond liner bubbling up in the centre, displacing the rocks and plants you painstakingly arranged. This situation is a classic example of hippoing caused by water accumulation under the liner as the groundwater pressure exceeds the weight of the water in your pond.

Understanding and addressing the risk of hippoing is crucial when choosing the right location for your pond. This initial effort in site selection will pay off, preventing problems and making the entire experience smoother.

Safety for Kids and Pets

Safety should always be a top priority when building a garden pond in a family setting without obstructing the view or the enjoyment of the space. The ideal pond location and design will add beauty and value to your garden and ensure that children, pets and visitors can enjoy it safely. I strongly recommend using physical barriers like fencing around the pond to create a safe environment, allowing you to relax while your kids and pets explore the garden.

Safety barriers have multiple benefits. They eliminate intrusive grids over the pond, ensuring your water lilies receive all the sunlight they need. In contrast, fish have full access to the surface to feed. Maintaining the pond is more manageable, and adults can supervise children and pets from a comfortable seating area. For those with pets, an interactive pond design can be a source of enrichment. My dog loves our ponds and has established favourite spots where she can observe or even cool off safely in the summer months. It's fascinating to watch the interactions between dogs and fish; these experiences can also be educational for children.

It's important to note that children who live at home are not always the most at risk; instead, their visiting friends might not be as familiar with the pond's presence or dangers. Fencing or barriers act as a precaution, reducing the risk of accidents. I explore this more in Chapter 9, "The Pond as a Family Project."

A few practical design solutions include adding rocks and gradual steps within the pond to make getting in and out more accessible for people and pets. Avoid using steep-sided ponds with bare liners, which can be challenging to navigate. Instead, build internal rockwork for easy access and stability. Many ponds I've serviced over the years had unsafe, sloping designs that even I found challenging to enter and exit safely. Incorporating flat rocks and submerged ledges can prevent these hazards and create a more family-friendly environment.

Safety grids are another practical solution, mainly if your pond is near a high-traffic area or play zone. Installing a blank safety grid beneath the surface can prevent accidental falls into deeper water. You can even integrate decorative metal artwork to cover ponds, adding an artistic flair without compromising safety.

The pond's location is just as important as its design for safety. Choose a spot that's easy to monitor from the house or garden seating areas. Avoid placing the pond near areas where kids frequently play, such as goalposts or trampolines. A pond too close to a play area can become an unintended hazard for curious children trying to retrieve items.

Safety Grid Behind a Goal

One of my memorable experiences involving pond safety occurred during a deep clean of a garden pond in Guilsborough, Northamptonshire. It was a small pond covered by a black plastic safety grid to keep kids and pets safe. The pond was situated at the top of a sloping garden, and right in the middle of a big lawn in front of it was a plastic football goal. This setup created unexpected concerns, but I thought it was okay as a temporary location here.

During the cleaning, I partially removed a small section of a black safety grid to access the pond, as I needed to vacuum out accumulated sludge. It was the school half-term, so when the family came home, their young son started kicking his football around the garden. That's when I discovered the goal had been placed here for the son to play!

Despite most of the safety grid being in place, I still felt uneasy because the goal was close to the pond. As I was tidying up, I noticed the boy standing at the pond's edge, nervously peering through the grid into the empty space beneath (as the water was in a holding tank). His football had landed on the grid, and he was unsure whether it was safe to step out and retrieve it. He asked me to get the ball for him.

After refilling the pond with water, I replaced the section I had removed, and the boy resumed his football game. When his ball landed on the grid this time, he didn't hesitate to step onto it, even though its strength hadn't changed. Seeing how his perception of safety shifted was fascinating because I had only just refilled the pond with water. The grid, which had looked dangerous over an empty pond, now seemed secure simply because the water was back.

This incident made me realise that while safety grids are crucial, they must be foolproof. The real issue was the placement of the pond in the middle of a large lawn (play area). It was a stark reminder to consider several options when planning a pond. This family didn't plan the pond, but relocating the football goal could have avoided the situation.

Even if all safety measures are in place, ponds should always be located away from active play areas to minimise risk.

Final Tips

These tips are meant to keep the pond beautiful, enjoyable and safe for everyone.

Take the time to walk around your garden and consider different viewpoints, aspects of your space and any nearby play areas or pathways. This will help you choose a beautiful and safe location for family members, pets and visitors.

Experiment by placing a garden hose or rope to outline the shape and size of the pond. This will help you visualise the placement, including safe access for maintenance and any necessary barriers for children or pets.

Remember that a well-placed pond can be a permanent addition to your landscape, so careful planning is essential to ensure it becomes a source of joy and safety, not frustration.

Take small steps. Begin with a manageable size for your first pond, considering how you will maintain and secure it. Later, as your confidence grows and your pond-building skills improve, you can expand, ensuring it remains an inviting and safe feature of your garden.

Your pond will become a cherished focal point in your garden – an oasis for you and local wildlife.

If you'd like more tips or need help deciding where to put your pond, join our growing community of pond enthusiasts. Visit https://waterfeature.shop/community to connect with like-minded pond lovers, share your ideas and get expert advice.

Chapter 3
TYPES OF PONDS FOR BEGINNERS

When choosing the type of pond that will suit your home, it's essential to balance the dream of a beautiful water feature with practical considerations. The ideal pond is one that not only complements your garden but also fits seamlessly into your lifestyle, budget and level of commitment to maintenance. By asking yourself simple questions, you can narrow your options and select a pond that will bring you joy for years without becoming a source of stress or regret.

Vital Points to Keep in Mind

Imagine the End Result

Take a moment to visualise the finished pond in your garden. What do you see? Are you picturing delicate lilies floating on still water, goldfish gliding around rocks or perhaps a wildlife pond attracting frogs, newts and dragonflies? It's easy to get excited about the possibilities, but consider whether the vision aligns with your space, budget and time. If you're jumping up and down with excitement, that's great! But remember, enthusiasm alone doesn't build a pond. This initial excitement can help you set the stage, but don't let it lead you into a more complex and costly project.

Creating a pond can be gratifying, transforming your garden into a vibrant, tranquil oasis. However, choosing the right pond type is crucial, as each type offers unique challenges and rewards. It's easy to get overwhelmed by the different options, but understanding how your brain works can help you make a better choice.

Make an Emotional Connection

Beyond the practical considerations, consider why you want a pond in the first place. Is it for the calming effect of running water? Is it to attract more wildlife to your garden? Or do you have fond memories of a pond from your childhood? Making this emotional connection will help guide you when the project becomes challenging, or decisions feel overwhelming. Sticking to your vision and staying motivated is more manageable if you have an apparent reason for building your pond.

Consider the Long-Term Commitment

Ponds are beautiful, but they require maintenance. Consider questions like: How much time are you willing to spend cleaning filters? If you need to go away, would you be okay with getting a house sitter to feed your fish? Do you love flowers? Will you find it therapeutic to trim and maintain plants?

A still wildlife pond or a simple frog pond might be the best choice if you want something cheap and low-maintenance (as they are most of the year). However, note that *you* are the mechanical filter with this type of pond. There is no maintenance help from internal filtration, but it is a lovely watering hole in your garden. Remember, we are here to help you create aquatic art to bring your garden to life.

If you want to keep the water crystal-clear for large koi carp, you'll need to prepare for more frequent attention, maintenance and investment in size and filtration equipment. This setup is more advanced and should only be attempted after enjoying a smaller pond. You will get frustrated if you start with koi. If you want colourful fish that stay small, pick shubunkins.

Five Pond Types for Beginners

When choosing the type of pond that suits your garden and lifestyle, consider your experience level, budget, available space and the amount of time you're willing to spend on maintenance.

Frog Pond (Easiest In-Ground)

With this type of pond, you're creating a haven for local wildlife and a space to watch tadpoles and frogs hop and croak. Imagine the joy of sitting next to a tiny pond alive with nature.

A frog pond can be created inexpensively and requires minimal maintenance. It does not need pumps or filters. Dig a shallow 30 cm-deep hole, line it, add rocks and plants, and let nature do the rest. You can get started right away!

I once built a small frog pond for a family who had just moved into their new home. They were worried it would take a lot of effort, but within a month, they had a thriving little ecosystem. Their young kids would race outside each morning to count the new frogs, and that small pond became a family focal point that created endless joy. But buy the right equipment carefully. It should be designed to last and not be disposable or cause problems down the line. A frog pond can be built in a single weekend. It requires little maintenance – just a seasonal clean-up to remove excess debris. It's perfect for nature lovers with limited time and space.

Maintenance Requirements

- Regularly skim leaves and debris from the surface by hand.
- Periodically check water levels, as small ponds evaporate more quickly.

- Ensure no harmful chemicals or excessive algae could affect the amphibian's health.
- Monitor and maintain plants to provide shade and hiding spots.
- If not appropriately managed, the pond may suffer overgrowth.

Potential Challenges

- Frog ponds can dry up quickly in the summer, so it's essential to top up water levels frequently.
- Never use chemicals to control algae, as they can harm amphibians.

Space Needed

- Small space, ideally **1 to 2 m²** (10 to 20 sq ft).

A frog pond is the least expensive pond type. Visit our website for more information: https://waterfeature.shop/frog-pond

Pot Pond (Limited Space)

Imagine having a tiny pond on your balcony or patio where miniature water lilies bloom in a small container. This quick way to add a touch of water magic to even the smallest space is ideal.

There's no need to worry about big digs or complicated equipment: just a watertight pot and a water plant or plants. Maintenance is simple and minimal, much less than bedding plants as you don't need to water every day. You can't overwater it and a complete pot pond project with a pump can be completed in a couple of hours.

One of my clients was a busy artist with little time for gardening. After we built her a beautiful wildlife pond with moving water, she set up a pot pond on her studio window ledge, which became an inspiration source. Watching the water's surface ripple in the wind as she worked helped her relax and feel more connected to nature. A blackbird even came for a bath one day in the small pot while she was painting right by the window. I bet it was a magical moment!

Some of these projects can be completed in minutes. You can enjoy a pot pond without needing pumps or filters, making it a manageable and early beginner-friendly option.

Maintenance Requirements

- Top up water levels regularly, as evaporation occurs quickly in small pots – more than in other garden pots.
- Remove dead leaves and plant debris to maintain water clarity.
- Apply liquid fertiliser for aquatic plants occasionally.

Potential Challenges

- Water can quickly become stagnant, leading to unpleasant odours or mosquito breeding if not maintained.

- Pot ponds have limited plant options due to space constraints.

Space Needed

- Minimal space will do – even something as small as a bucket **30cm** (1 sq ft).
- These can be placed on a windowsill, balcony or table in any miniature garden area.

Pot Ponds are not at all expensive. Visit our website for more information: https://waterfeature.shop/pot-pond.

Still Wildlife Pond (Nature)

If you love attracting double the amount of wildlife to your garden, such as a few damselflies (maybe the odd dragonfly), garden birds and an array of amphibians, a still wildlife pond is perfect. You can create a small oasis that brings nature right to your doorstep. This type of pond is natural and undemanding. Maintenance is straightforward and does not require complex equipment. All you need to do is dig a hole, add a liner and some small native aquatic plants, and let nature work its magic.

When a friend felt down about his divorce, I invited him for a beer. It was very nice to show him around my garden. My ponds inspired him and briefly took his mind off his problems.

I had just finished building a substantial still-wildlife pond and ended up giving him an offcut I would have used for another pond build or as a kit cover. He went back to his mum's house and, using the offcut, built a pond for him and his kids. Even on a tight budget, he was able to create a still-water wildlife pond that quickly became a source of fascination and relaxation.

I remember sitting in his mum's garden one afternoon, watching him enjoy the pond he had created with grass edges and some purple bricks he had collected. He said, "It does not have to be that complicated." He told me his kids made a beeline for it every time they came around and were excited as they discovered new creatures making the pond their home.

Maintenance Requirements

- Regularly clear out fallen leaves and organic debris to prevent buildup.
- Thin out fast-growing plants annually to maintain balance.
- Add beneficial bacteria to help break down organic matter and maintain water quality.

Potential Challenges

- Too much organic matter can make the pond murky and affect water quality.
- If not correctly managed, stagnant water can become a breeding ground for mosquitoes (You need wildlife – dragonflies love eating mosquitoes!).

Space Needed

- A minimum of **2 to 4 m²** (20 to 40 sq ft) is sufficient enough for a balanced habitat.

A still wildlife pond costs little, but invest in the best materials for long-term enjoyment. Visit our website for more information: https://waterfeature.shop/still-pond

Small Fish Pond (Small Fish)

Imagine colourful goldfish gliding through crystal-clear water. A small fish pond adds life and movement to your garden, creating a serene atmosphere where you can unwind and enjoy the gentle splashing sounds. Start small with a kit. A fish pond can be as straightforward or complex as you want it to be. Maintaining a small fish pond is more manageable than you might think with the correct setup and a little care.

As I write this, all sorts of memories are popping up. One memorable gentleman had reached out to me after watching a few of my videos; we exchanged a couple of emails back and forth, and he wanted to spend more time outside. He told me he had just lost his wife and was having mental health issues, but was keen to start a new project. We talked for a while, and I recommended a small fish pond, which he rebuilt a few times (Good, Better, and Best). It was fantastic to hear that his doctor had prescribed that he spend some of his money on a gardening project. He would send pictures of it. Over time, the fish had babies, so he wanted help upgrading filters and determining which plants to grow. He expanded it into a beautiful, multi-tiered water garden within a few years. His pond became the heart of his garden, where he could relax and feel at peace.

If you want low maintenance, invest in more extensive filters, as this depends on the size and equipment needed. Our primary small fish pond kit includes a pump and filter to keep the water clean. With this setup, expect to spend a few hours each season on maintenance, like cleaning the filter and checking water quality. It's ideal for those who want a dynamic garden feature without taking on too much at once. For other setups, you can look at weekly maintenance, so shop wisely, as the price can be misleading. If it's too cheap, ask why and read the small print.

Maintenance Requirements

- Clean the filter and pump regularly, depending on your setup and design.
- Remove uneaten fish food and excess algae.
- Perform partial water changes to maintain water quality (if you don't have enough rain).
- Sometimes, you must test water quality and balance pH, ammonia and nitrate levels.

Potential Challenges

- Fish are sensitive to changes in water quality and require more attention.

- These ponds can be more prone to algae growth due to adding fish food, which turns into nutrient levels in the water.

Space Needed

- You'll need a minimum of **4 to 6 m^2** (40 to 60 sq ft), with a depth of at least 60 cm (2 ft), for fish comfort.

A small fish pond kit costs more than others. Visit our website for more information: https://waterfeature.shop/fish-pond

Small Water Garden (Plants-Only Ponds)

A small water garden filled with vibrant plants like water lilies and iris can turn a corner of your garden into a colourful sanctuary. The blooms and greenery will draw your eye and lift your spirits. Unlike a fish pond, there's no need to worry about keeping fish healthy or the additional cost of filters. Water gardens focus on plants, making them less complex to maintain.

A past client created a small water garden near her back door. Each morning, she'd take her coffee outside and watch the lilies open, enjoying her created peaceful environment. I remember talking to her and laughing when she told me that the problem with plants is that they grow. It's incredible. With the correct setup and plant selection, you will be giving them away. I refer to them as kids; you try to get them to talk and walk for the first couple of years, and then you wish they would shut up and sit down.

Maintenance Requirements

- Maintenance involves plant husbandry and topping up water levels. For husbandry, follow my four Ds: Removing "dead, dying, diseased" foliage and "detail," or trimming plants back to tidy them up.
- No pumps or filtration are required, making it perfect for beginners who want a manageable water feature.
- Regularly trim and thin out aquatic plants to prevent overgrowth.
- Check water levels and replenish as needed.
- Remove plant material to maintain water clarity and avoid decay.

Potential Challenges

- Overgrowth can make maintenance easier if managed regularly.
- Some plants might become invasive, requiring constant trimming or netting out.

Space Needed

- Depending on the number and size of plants, you may need **3 to 6 m²** (30 to 60 sq ft).

These setup costs vary widely depending on the number and type of plants. Visit our website for more information: https://waterfeature.shop/plant-pond.

Recap: The Right Pond Recipe for the Beginner

Frog Ponds. These are ideal for beginners with minimal space. They require the least maintenance and cost among in-ground ponds, and they are a great starting point for nature lovers looking to support local wildlife.

Patio Pots. are perfect for those with limited space or who want to add a water feature to their balcony or patio. They are low-cost and easy to maintain, but their scope for aquatic life is limited.

Still Wildlife Ponds. These are a good option for those interested in a naturalistic garden feature. They are easy to maintain and focus on attracting wildlife like birds, frogs and beneficial insects.

Fish Ponds. These are for those interested in keeping small fish like goldfish. They require more maintenance and a slightly higher budget for filtration and equipment.

Small Water Gardens. These are best for plant enthusiasts who want to showcase a variety of aquatic plants. Maintenance involves regular trimming and seasonal care.

Five Advanced Systems (The Next Level)

These are for experienced pond builders or those willing to invest in a complex pond. They have a high budget and more maintenance requirements but are rewarding for serious hobbyists.

Ecosystem or Koi Ponds

These ponds recreate a balanced natural ecosystem with fish, plants and beneficial bacteria. They require more planning and effort but can be autonomous with the correct setup. They are the ultimate for fish lovers. Koi require deep water, heavy-duty filtration and more attention to water quality.

Professionally installed features or aquatic art can cost four to seven figures, depending on the scale and equipment needed for the project.

For a rough idea about the cost of hiring a professional, see our water feature menu at https://waterfeature.menu/collections/ponds.

Maintenance

- Monitor and maintain water quality through regular testing and adjustments.
- Clean out skimmers or mechanical filters monthly (as needed).
- Check for leaks or damage to plumbing, pumps and other equipment.
- Prune more plants and manage fish health more frequently.

Potential Challenges

- Both systems require more commitment and expertise to design and build for balanced water conditions.
- Equipment and running costs can be much higher due to different factors, such as filtration and aeration needs.

Space Needed

- **Koi ponds:** At least **15 m²** (150 sq ft) will do, with a depth of just under a meter 90 cm (3 ft).
- **Ecosystem ponds:** Depending on design and plant life, they should be at least **4 to 8 m²** (40 to 80 sq ft).

Rainwater Harvesting Ponds

These eco-friendly ponds are ideal for those looking to incorporate sustainable water management. Because this modular system collects rainwater to fill and sustain ponds and water gardens, it can be more technical and require water collection and distribution planning. Although it's environmentally friendly, setup costs can be high due to the need for underground storage basins and advanced plumbing.

Maintenance

- Regularly check water levels and ensure no overflow or dry spells.

- Inspect pipes and gutters for blockages and clean the rainwater filters to keep debris from the system or pond.
- You need a sustainable water feature to keep the water reasonable.
- Test the water quality to ensure the rainwater is safe for fish or plants.

Potential Challenges

- They tend to be weather-dependent. It may dry out during prolonged dry spells without additional water sources.
- It can introduce pollutants from roof surfaces into the pond.

Space Needed

- These need **2 to 6m² plus** (20 to 60+ sq ft) or more, depending on the volume of water you want to harvest.

These can be small or right up to substantial commercial projects.

Sparkling Wildlife Ponds

These are beautiful additions for those who love the sound of moving water. They add life and sound to the garden but require more maintenance for pumps and filters. Better filtration and moving water enhance a wildlife pond. Moving the water prevents stagnation and doubles the amount of wildlife again compared to still water (so you can have four times more wildlife), but it requires a pump and power source. You must have the correct setup to move water around in a wildlife pond safely. Don't just install a pond pump in the bottom of a pond; these are not wildlife-friendly (even when they say they are).

Maintenance

- Regularly clean and maintain the filters and features like waterfalls, streams and spitters (ornamental water features).
- Check for blockages from plants and algae growth in the moving water areas.

Potential Challenges

- Moving water features can attract more leaves and debris (as the surface is usually more significant due to streams or waterfalls, which can clog the system).
- The sound of water might need to be controlled to avoid excessive noise.
- Electrical installations might be required if they are not close by, but solar options are getting better (depending on the feature size).

Space Needed

- Allot **2 to 8 m^2** (20 to 80 sq ft), with space for water features like small waterfalls or streams.

Duck Ponds

These are suitable for those with more significant properties who want to raise ducks or have a pond that can handle a high organic load. They are also high-maintenance due to waste management. Ornamental duck ponds are designed to be clean and clear (they get so much more joy from them, as do you), focusing on filtration. Ducks can be messy, so heavy-duty filters are required to maintain water quality. If you see a duck pond, it's usually green and smells, but it doesn't have to be this way. To handle the high organic load from ducks, you need the correct filtration system (wetland and intake bay) and regularly clean and maintain filters and pumps.

Maintenance

- Check water levels and top up as needed.
- Remove excess duck waste to prevent water quality issues.
- Help the aquatic plants survive the hungry mouths and nest builders.

Potential Challenges

- Ducks' high organic load can make water quality management challenging.
- Maintaining clear water requires heavy-duty filtration and cleaning.

Space Needed

- Two ducks need at least **8 to 10 m²** (80 to 100 sq ft) to swim comfortably.

Swim Ponds and Plunge Pools

These are for those who want a natural swimming experience. Swim ponds and plunge pools are the most expensive and maintenance-intensive, but they offer unique enjoyment and relaxation as they are designed for human interaction. They require specialised construction, advanced filtration and regular maintenance, making them a high-cost but rewarding feature for those looking to merge garden aesthetics with personal use.

Maintenance

- Clean wetland filters and skimmers or intake bays regularly to keep the water clear.
- Remove leaves and debris to maintain water quality.

Potential Challenges

- More attention is required to water chemistry and regular maintenance.
- It can be costly to run, especially with heating.
- When designing for human immersion, there must not be any main power underwater for water movement.
- These types of ponds are best for those with experience or willing to hire a professional due to the higher costs and build complexity.

Space Needed

- **Swim ponds:** For swimming comfort, they should be at least **40 to 45 m²** (400 to 450 square feet) and at least **1.2 to 1.5 m** (4 to 5 ft) deep.
- **Plunge pools:** They can be smaller, around **6 to 10 m²** (60 to 100 sq ft), and have a depth of **90 cm to 1.2 m** (3 to 4 ft).

Selecting the Right Pond for You

Choosing the perfect pond type depends on your goals, available space and budget. Whether you dream of a serene wildlife haven, a vibrant fish pond or a tranquil water garden, the key is to start small and build your confidence before exploring more complex options.

For beginners, simplicity is your ally. A ready-to-install pond kit can take the guesswork out of your project, providing everything you need for a functional and long-lasting feature. These kits are designed to be easy to use, giving you a professional result without the frustration of mismatched components or unforeseen challenges.

Investing in a pond kit might mean a slightly higher initial cost, but it saves you time, prevents costly mistakes and ensures your pond brings joy for years. We've stocked our online store, Water Feature Shop, with beginner-friendly pond kits that have been tried and tested over the decades to help you get started with confidence. Explore your options at https://waterfeature.shop/beginner-pond-kits.

Chapter 4
PLANNING AND DESIGNING YOUR POND

Welcome to one of the most crucial stages of your pond-building journey: planning and designing. A well-thought-out pond doesn't just look stunning; it ensures long-term success, is easier to maintain and brings endless joy. We've already discussed the joys and benefits of owning a pond, choosing the perfect spot and the types of ponds for beginners. But before you start digging, there are vital questions you might not even know you should be asking. This chapter guides you through the critical planning and design stages, ensuring your pond fits your space, lifestyle and long-term vision. You can choose the most straightforward options of a pond kit unless your vision demands something complex.

When planning and designing a pond, it's easy for beginners to get overwhelmed by the variety of options and materials available. Some people overcomplicate the process, while others recommend building everything to perfection, which can unnecessarily inflate costs. Without proper planning, creating a pond is like cooking without a recipe – you might end up with something, but it won't be what you envisioned (unless you're a pro). Proper planning prevents costly mistakes, such as poorly selected or unnecessary materials or insufficient equipment. It's about getting it right the first time so you don't end up with a pond that's hard to maintain or fails. Save yourself time, energy and money by planning correctly.

Think of this chapter as your pond-building roadmap. By breaking it down step-by-step, I'll help you make the most of your investment, time and space.

Choose the Right Building Style

Flexible Pond Liners (Recommended for Beginners)

Flexible pond liners are among the most versatile and beginner-friendly options. Typically made from PVC or EPDM rubber, they allow you to create ponds of any shape or size. Rubber is ideal if you're unsure of your final pond design or plan to expand it later. You can easily shape the liner to fit curved or irregular layouts, and it provides a reliable, waterproof bag that can be very simple or more complex.

Advantages

- **Easy to install.** Flexible pond liners are relatively simple to install, even for beginners. They allow for creative freedom in the shape and size of the pond.
- **Expandable.** Because rubber liners are flexible, you can upgrade or expand the pond in the future by simply adding another liner with a primmer and tape (beginners need not worry about that at the moment; we are not cutting out sections or glueing sections on to start with).
- **Cost-effective.** PVC liners are a budget-friendly choice because of their size and flexibility. They are very affordable in the short term.

Maintenance

These liners require protective matting to prevent punctures from sharp rocks or tree roots (long-term). Some companies recommend an underlay at a minimum to keep the cost down. However, I recommend a double layer of protective matting, which provides cheap insurance against long-term punctures.

Challenges

A double layer of protective matting can prevent the liner from being punctured by damage, wildlife, roots or sharp stones. Proper coverage is also necessary to hide the liner and to avoid wear.

Pre-Formed Pools (Plastic or Fibreglass)

Pre-formed pools are primarily rigid, pre-shaped liners typically made from plastic or fibreglass. Some are self-supporting and of excellent quality (others could be better and more attractive). The good ones are straightforward for beginners who want a rapid set-up and are not worried about the shape or recreating nature. These ponds have a long life expectancy and do not suffer from unsightly creases (like bare-liner ponds). They are only sometimes wildlife friendly as the smooth sides are hard to climb, plus edging them is much harder traditionally with slabs. They come in various sizes and depths, usually with built-in shelves for plants. Pre-formed ponds are perfect for smaller gardens and work well on hard-standing areas (which you can't dig).

Advantages

- **Quick installation.** The self-supporting options are quick to install (once in your garden) and go on a solid base. There is no need to shape or mould the pond – just drop it on a level surface and fill it with water.
- **Durable.** The fibreglass versions are extremely tough and resistant to damage, which means less maintenance over time.
- **Water Loss.** Solid plastic or fibreglass liners have less chance of punctures or leaks from low edges.

Maintenance

Preformed ponds are relatively low-maintenance. However, due to their formal shape with dead spots or pumps in the base, they require more maintenance. You will need to occasionally clean and net out waste that does get filtered out, such as leaves. Over the long term, fibreglass versions may require less attention than plastic ones.

Challenges

You're limited by the pre-set shape and size. These units are more challenging to install unless they are self-supporting. This can make it hard to customise the pond to your specific garden layout. Also, larger pre-formed ponds can be challenging to transport and install due to their weight and rigidity. If you are not careful, the whole pond might sink into the ground, giving you large areas of exposed fibreglass. Edging these pools is very hard as you don't tend to use rocks to naturalise the inside; the best ones I have seen were installed on large concrete pads.

Concrete Ponds (Block and Render)

Concrete ponds are a professional option for creating fish farming conditions, as well as koi pools or formal water gardens. They're built using concrete blocks, then rendered and waterproofed, making them incredibly durable. These ponds are often designed with deep, straight edges or geometric shapes and can be integrated into modern garden designs or formal landscapes. One obstacle in my concrete pool was subsidence under the foundation created by seasonal changes. I had to drop in a flexible liner when the block work cracked, a repair that was quite costly.

Advantages

- **High-end appearance.** These water features offer a more polished, formal look and can be customised with built-in features like seating areas, rills or integrated lighting.
- **Large size.** Concrete ponds accommodate large volumes of water, making them ideal for koi or extensive water gardens.

Maintenance

Concrete ponds are durable but require regular maintenance to prevent algae growth and ensure water quality, especially if you keep fish. The concrete can also crack over time, especially in colder climates, so annual inspections are recommended.

Challenges

Building a pond is significantly more expensive and time-consuming than building flexible liners or preformed ponds. You'll also need professional or advanced DIY skills to ensure the pond is built correctly and the waterproofing is effective.

Which Building Style Is Right for You?

Let's break down the options so you can choose one that best fits your vision, needs and budget. Each style has advantages, whether it's a flexible liner, pre-formed pool or concrete pond. Pick a style that fits your budget, space and maintenance capabilities.

Pond Style	Installation Difficulty	Budget	Ideal For	Wildlife/ Aquatic Life	Material Maintenance
Flexible Pond Liner	Easy to moderate	Low to premium	Beginners, most garden sizes	Can be made custom, wildlife friendly	Low (with protection)
Pre-Formed Ponds	Easy to moderate	Low to medium	Limited space, fast setup	Small fish, insects	Low (fibreglass)
Concrete Ponds	Difficult	High	Formal gardens	Large fish, koi	High (long-term)

Key Points to Remember

Flexible pond liners offer customisation. Flexible liners are the most versatile and beginner-friendly option. They allow for creative freedom in design and can easily be expanded or upgraded over time.

Pre-formed pools are quick to install. If you're looking for a fast setup and don't mind limited design flexibility, pre-formed plastic or fibreglass ponds are durable and require minimal installation effort with a suitable base.

Concrete ponds are durable but require investment. While they are long-lasting and ideal for large fish like koi, they need more time, money, and skills to build and maintain.

Ask Yourself Practical Questions

Once you've identified the type of pond that excites you, it's time to get practical. Here are key questions to ask yourself.

What Size Pond is Manageable?

A larger pond provides more stability but will also require more maintenance. A smaller pond is more accessible to care for but may limit your options for plants and fish. When deciding on the size of your pond, it's essential to consider the trade-offs. A larger pond offers more space for fish and plants, providing more environmental stability, but requires more maintenance and a bigger budget. On the other hand, a smaller pond or patio water feature is easier to manage and more cost-effective. Consider your priorities and resources when determining the ideal size for your pond.

Kate's Pond Build

My friend Kate is a passionate young gardener dreaming about creating a small pond in her new home. She felt overwhelmed about where to start and initially considered hiring a professional but did not have the budget. However, after seeing my posts on Facebook and watching my step-by-step wildlife pond-building videos, she decided to tackle the project herself as she wanted frogs to eat the slugs. With the help of my Frog Pond Kit, Kate found the process manageable and enjoyable, from laying out the shape to placing all the rocks, stones and waterplant pouches for a peaceful wildlife sanctuary next to her vegetable patch. The kit saved her time, fit her budget and boosted her confidence.

A month later, she added a small pond pump for the soothing sound of water, using my simple double pot method, which she had learned in one of my videos. It keeps the tadpoles safe from being sucked into the pump. Kate enjoys sharing her success with fellow gardeners on Facebook and even helped a friend create a budget-friendly wildlife pond.

Kate's story proves that, with the proper guidance, even beginners can create a beautiful, thriving pond that brings lasting joy.

Kate advises anyone looking to start their pond journey: *"Don't overthink it. Watch the videos, follow the steps and just go for it! You'll be amazed at what you can accomplish, and you don't need to hire a professional to create something exceptional."*

Her success story reminds us that with the proper guidance, even a beginner can create a beautiful, thriving pond that will bring joy to their garden for years to come.

What is My Budget?

Be realistic about how much you are willing to invest. Larger and more complex ponds require bigger budgets, not just for the initial build but also for ongoing maintenance. It's crucial to prioritise your expenses based on your goals. For example, some people may prefer to invest more in high-quality, beautiful fish while paying less attention to the pond's aesthetics. In contrast, others might focus on creating a visually stunning pond with more straightforward fish. Determining your budget and priorities upfront allows you to make better decisions throughout your pond project.

If cost is a concern, consider starting with a simpler pond and expanding as your budget allows. Investing in a professionally designed pond kit is one way to avoid costly mistakes. These kits include all the essential materials, such as the correct-size liner, pumps and filtration systems.

Common mistakes – like selecting the wrong liner size or inadequate filtration – can lead to expensive problems down the line. Spending more upfront on a well-planned kit will save you money by preventing these issues and ensuring long-term success.

How Much Time Are You Able to Commit to the Project?

Are you interested in a weekend project or are you willing to spend several months perfecting your pond? Some systems take longer to build and require regular attention, while others are more hands-off. When deciding how much time to dedicate to your pond project, consider the level of commitment required.

More complex designs with intricate details also take longer to perfect. However, it's possible to build a pond within a day or a weekend and only spend half a day managing it annually. Using a pond kit developed by a professional can significantly reduce construction time, although it's essential to be aware of the kit's limitations. This approach can save valuable time and effort, allowing you to enjoy your pond more quickly.

Where Will the Pump, Filter and Power Source Be?

Plan for easy access to these critical components so maintenance won't be a chore later. A well-designed filtration system can save you hours of work.

When planning the layout for your pond, consider the placement of the pump, filter and power source for easy access during maintenance. A well-designed filtration system can save you valuable time and effort in the long run. Consider placing the filter on one side and the pump on the other, and incorporate a skim cove to collect floating debris.

Square corners, for instance, can create "dead spots" where water movement is minimal, allowing debris and algae to build up. These stagnant areas can lead to poor water quality, requiring more maintenance and cleaning.

On the other hand, curved edges promote smoother water flow, which helps with natural filtration and keeps debris circulating towards your pond's skimmer or filter. Although curves may be more challenging to construct, especially for beginners, they offer aesthetic and functional benefits. A curved pond not only looks more natural and visually appealing, but it also helps maintain healthier water by encouraging better circulation. In the long run, opting for a curved shape will save you time and effort in maintaining a cleaner, well-balanced pond ecosystem.

Regarding depth, it's essential to strike a balance. Fish don't get the exercise they need from swimming up and down, similar to how a bird expends energy taking off or landing. Most garden ponds ranging from 50 cm to 1 m in depth are suitable for fish and the overall ecosystem.

What Filtration System Will You Need?

The pond type – whether for fish, frogs or human enjoyment – dictates its filtration needs. Fish ponds need robust systems to handle waste, while wildlife ponds may only need minimal filtration. Match your filtration system to your pond's size and function to avoid maintenance headaches later. A well-designed filtration system saves time and maintenance in the long run.

Ensure your filtration system matches your pond. A well-designed filtration system saves time and maintenance in the long run. Match your filter to your pond's size and function, whether for fish, frogs or straightforward water enjoyment.

Plan for easy maintenance. Whether you're deciding where to place the pump and filter or determining the shape of the pond, careful planning now will save you time and effort on maintenance later.

Strategies for Building a Stunning Pond on a Limited Budget

You don't need to spend a fortune to create a beautiful pond. You can repurpose materials where possible (though I would not recommend using a second-hand liner). If you're on a budget or new to pond building, start with a smaller pond and expand later. This allows you to avoid costly mistakes and gain confidence as you go.

Saving Money With Second-Hand Materials and DIY Techniques

On my first pond, I used second-hand materials wherever I could. I repurposed old bricks, garden slabs and plastic pipes for fish caves, used hair curlers and plastic pot scourers as filter media, and received second-hand pumps from friends. This saved money and gave my pond a unique, personal touch. Small touches like these can make a big difference when working on a tight budget.

I learned a lot from my first pond, especially regarding the effectiveness of filtration systems. Initially, I needed to understand mechanical and biological filtration differences fully. I had a traditional pond pump placed at the bottom, which quickly became problematic with the tiny sponges blocking up almost daily, resulting in me adding more pumps. At times, leaves would block them up. They all pulled waste into hard-to-reach areas, making cleaning a nightmare. Eventually, I switched to a more efficient system with a pump in a large box, but this was a nightmare when it was time to clean it. Most of the waste could not be removed, so we would have to net it out.

My first pond always seemed to have problems, which multiplied as I tried to understand and beat the premium filters. One morning, I came up to my pond and found it making a crazy noise. I discovered that my filter had been leaking, resulting in the entire pond emptying unexpectedly.

Through trial and error, I realised that having the right filtration system, like biological filters designed to process clean water free of organic matter, was vital in maintaining water clarity and fish health.

Since 2013, I have only installed solid handling pumps in fish pools (or fish farming setups, as this is the only fish waste we deal with on the bottom). The rest must be in skimmers, intake bays or skim coves. These help pull debris from the surface before it sinks, preventing any build-up at the bottom.

Tips for Creating a Pond Without Overspending

Choose simple designs. Start with a basic pond layout and add features as your budget allows.

Repurpose materials. Use old bricks, free rockery stones (from marketplaces), or even a large flower pot. Many beginner pond owners use second-hand materials like vintage bathtubs, plastic plant containers or oak barrels (note: whiskey barrels still need a liner) as pond bases. They're inexpensive and give the pond a charming, rustic look.

Use DIY filters. Instead of buying a premium filter system, build a DIY filter using larger food-safe storage containers, a simple pump and some aquatic-safe gravel.

Gary's Story

So, I've got a heartwarming story about one of my clients whom I think you'll love. It's about Gary, an electrical engineer who wanted to do something special for his grandmother's birthday. Instead of going for something extravagant, he created a little oasis for her – a small fish pond that perfectly captured her love for nature. Even more impressive is how he kept it simple and low-maintenance, ensuring she could enjoy it without fuss. He focused on simplicity, resisting the urge to add unnecessary features, and stayed true to what his grandmother wanted: a peaceful space she could enjoy every day.

Gary's personal touch was repurposing an old flat stone with sentimental value – a keepsake from his late grandfather. With care, he placed it at the pond's edge to create a feeding rock, creating a serene spot for his grandmother to relax and feed the fish. She even used her handmade leaf scoop (a flour sieve attached to a garden cane), showing how simplicity and personal touches can go a long way.

The pond quickly became a cherished feature in her garden. It wasn't just a decorative addition; it became a tranquil retreat for the entire family. Gary's young daughter, who faced mental health challenges, found calm and contentment sitting by the pond, feeding the fish from the unique stone.

Gary's story shows how focusing on what truly matters – meeting practical needs while adding a personal touch – can create a pond that brings lasting joy. It's easy to get caught up in aiming for perfection or complex designs, but the best pond is one that fits your life and brings satisfaction for years to come. Keep your project simple, meaningful and aligned with your vision.

Using Native Plants to Design a Low-Maintenance Pond

For low-maintenance pond design (still or moving), choose native plants that naturally thrive in your local environment. In the UK, plants like common water plantain (*Alisma plantago-aquatica*), Sweet Galingale (*Cyperus longus*) native water lilies and miniature varieties are excellent choices. These water plants help by filtering the water, reducing algae growth, absorbing excess nutrients, reducing the need for treatments or frequent cleaning and providing shelter for wildlife. Water lilies add vibrant colour and shade, which helps regulate water temperature and minimise algae growth. In contrast, miniature water plantain (*Alisma parviflora*) is perfect for small pot ponds, providing beauty and attracting beneficial insects without overwhelming limited spaces. Together, these plants create a balanced, eco-friendly pond that requires minimal upkeep, making your pond easier to care for year-round.

When planning and designing your pond, ensuring your filtration system is practical and appropriately sized for its intended purpose is crucial. The type of pond – whether for fish, frogs or simply for human enjoyment – dictates the filtration needs. Fish ponds require more robust filtration to handle waste and maintain water clarity, while wildlife ponds with frogs may need only minimal filtration to support a natural ecosystem. For human immersion, like swimming ponds, filtration must be even more extensive to maintain cleanliness. I would not recommend this be tackled as your first pond, however.

Planning and designing your pond doesn't have to be complicated. By asking yourself the right questions, choosing the right type for your lifestyle and investing in quality materials, you'll be well on your way to creating a pond that enhances your garden and brings joy for years.

DIY Upgrades for Small Garden or Pot Ponds

Implementing several straightforward strategies can significantly enhance a small pond. Explore these effective methods to transform your pond into a stunning focal point.

Aeration. A solar-powered aerator is perfect for small fish ponds or wildlife ponds. It helps keep the water oxygenated, and it's ideal for beginners because it's low-maintenance, eco-friendly and easy to set up.

Water Features. Add a decorative element with a solar-powered spitter. Spitters, which come in various shapes, such as frogs or turtles, gently circulate the water, helping prevent stagnation while adding charm.

Lighting. Solar-powered pond lights are easy to install for evening pond enjoyment and are perfect for beginners. Use them to illuminate water lilies, fish or decorative features, enhancing your pond's visual appeal at night.

The Value of Investing in a Beginner Pond Kit

Throughout this chapter, we've explored how thoughtful planning, practical design choices and intelligent use of resources can set you up for pond-building success. If you're a beginner, avoiding the trial-and-error process is essential to ensure your first pond is functional and enjoyable.

A beginner pond kit is your shortcut to success. These thoughtfully designed kits include all the essential components, such as a properly sized liner, a reliable pump, and an effective filtration system to skip the guesswork. With everything included, you can build confidently, knowing that each part is compatible and designed for long-term durability.

For first-time pond builders, simplicity is vital. You can use standard gardening tools with these kits to create a stunning pond without needing advanced technical skills. They're also engineered to avoid common pitfalls like leaks, undersized filters and debris build-up, giving you a worry-free start.

Think of a beginner pond kit as an investment in your pond and peace of mind. Starting with the right tools and a solid foundation will save time, energy and money, allowing you to focus on what matters most: enjoying the tranquillity and beauty of your new pond.

Ready to take the next step? Explore our range of beginner pond kits at https://waterfeature.shop/beginner-pond-kits and start your pond journey with confidence.

Chapter 5
STEP-BY-STEP POND INSTALLATIONS

It's time to stop dreaming and start digging. In this chapter, I'll walk you through creating your ideal pond, whether it's a serene frog pond, a vibrant fish pond or an elegant water garden. Think of this chapter as your "recipe card" for pond installation with easy-to-follow steps for each type of pond – and sprinkled with creative solutions to common challenges. I'll cover the key steps, from digging and lining to the finishing touches, that will make your pond look professional, even if you're a beginner.

This chapter combines three "step-by-step guides" for three different types of ponds with professional advice on making the ponds look great, even for beginners. Remember, enjoy the process. Building a pond is a journey. Don't rush; instead, relish the moments of creation and learning.

Consider a beginner pond kit if you're at the planning stage and haven't gathered materials yet. These kits are designed to streamline the process by including everything you need, from liner and protective matting to plant pouches and essential tools. Starting with a curated kit lets you skip the hassle of sourcing individual components and enjoy the creative process right from the start.

Beginner's Guide to Building a Serene Frog Pond

At the start of your pond project, make sure you have everything you need! Use this checklist to gather the tools, materials and equipment you need for a smooth installation.

Pond Kit Size

- Check the size of your pond kit to ensure you're digging to the correct dimensions
- Confirm your kit's correct liner size and pond depth - typically 30 to 60 cm (12 to 24 inches)

Materials

- Flexible pond liner: The correct size is based on your pond kit
- Protective matting: Enough to cover both under and over the liner

- Aquatic safe stones: Gravels, pebbles and small rocks create a natural look and provide shallow areas and shelter for frogs.
- Water garden pouches: To hold aquatic plants and soil in place
- Aquatic plants: Native plants such as miniature water lilies and marginal plants
- Safe water source: Half rainwater and half tap water (or Pond Detoxifier for dechlorinating tap water)
- Pond detoxifier: To neutralise chlorine in tap water.
- Multi aqua sachets: To introduce beneficial bacteria for pond health
- Multi clear: To prevent algae growth and maintain water clarity

Tools

- Spade or shovel: For digging and shaping the pond
- Sharp knife or scissors: Used to cut the liner and protective matting to size
- Spirit level (Ideally 1800mm): To ensure the pond is level and sits properly in your garden
- Tape measure: This is for accurate pond size and depth measurements.
- Wheelbarrow: To transport soil, rocks and materials around the garden
- Garden hose: This can mark the pond shape and fill it with tap water

Optional Natural Elements

- Driftwood or deadwood: This creates climbing spots and extra frog sheltering.
- Terracotta pots: Broken pieces to create caves and frog shelters

Final Check

Ensure you have enough space cleared and the area is level. Next, view the pond's shape from different viewpoints in your garden. Lastly, double-check that all materials and tools are ready for each installation step.

Step-by-Step Guide to Creating a Serene Frog Pond

1. Mark Out the Pond Area

Clear the area. Start by removing grass, weeds or plants from the pond area. Use a shovel or rake to clear the surface of the soil, ensuring no rocks, sticks or other debris could interfere with digging. Check for obstacles, such as tree roots or large stones, which may need to be shifted or removed entirely.

Shape the pond with a garden hose. Lay the garden hose where you want the pond's perimeter. Bend and curve the hose to create an organic, natural shape, ideal for a frog pond. Avoid straight lines or rigid shapes for a more visually appealing and wildlife-friendly design. Once satisfied with the shape, measure the area to ensure it fits the pond kit specifications. Make adjustments as needed. Check the measurements for the footprint of the pond and note the maximum length and width (see pond kit for size limits).

Check and mark the ground level. Use a spirit level to assess the ground's evenness across the marked area. Identify high spots that need digging and low areas that should be filled. Mark these areas with stakes or string. For sloped areas, ensure that the pond will sit at a level. This is crucial for maintaining proper water flow and preventing uneven drainage. Double-check the level after marking the ground to confirm that adjustments have been made correctly.

Final check. Walk around the marked pond area from various angles, including different viewing spots in your garden (such as from the house or patio). This will give you an overall sense of how the pond fits into the space and looks within the broader garden context. Ensure that the shape looks natural and is positioned to enhance the garden, making any final adjustments to the shape or location if necessary.

2. Excavate the Pond

Now that the area is marked, it's time to dig!

Depth. The depth of your pond will largely depend on the specific pond kit you have chosen. Aim for a shallow depth of just 30 cm (12 in) for the small frog pond kit. For medium and extensive kits, you'll excavate to depths of 45 cm and 60 cm (approximately 18 to 24 in). This depth is perfect for creating a healthy European Frog Pond, as it mirrors the shallow, temporary water bodies in which these amphibians naturally thrive. Their Latin name, *Rana temporaria* reflects their affinity for such temporary water sources, emphasising the importance of shallow, easily accessible ponds for these frogs.

Gently sloping sides. It is essential to design your pond with gently sloping sides or at least sloping rocks. While European frogs tend to avoid basking in the sun, they still appreciate shallow areas for swimming. Consider allowing for a gradual slope on at least one side of the pond (this is not a bare liner, however). This will make it easier for frogs to enter and exit the water and assist with maintenance.

Create levels. To enhance the ecological habitat of your frog pond, dig one or two shelves for ledges for the plants and rocks around the edge. These levels provide shelter and resting areas for frogs and add visual interest and depth to your pond design.

3. Install the Protective Matting and Liner

Make your pond waterproof.

Check the surface. Make sure the pond floor and sides of the hole are smooth and free of sharp objects. Add sand or extra protective matting to cover rough spots.

Add the first protective layer. Once you're happy, lay the first layer of protective matting into the excavation. A large single piece is best as the matting shields the liner, which you can't get below once the liner is in. Ensure it's snug and fully covers the floor and sides. On large ponds, overlap the sheets to stop or slow tree roots.

Add the pond liner. Smooth the flexible liner over the matting, then allow it to settle for 10 to 15 minutes.

Add the second protective layer. Lay another matting layer over the liner, using rocks and plant pouches to hold it.

4. Create Areas That Frogs Will Love

Enhance the habitat for your frog friends.

For European frogs, focus on creating shaded areas with rocks, submerged logs and aquatic plants that provide cover and shelter. Unlike some American species that bask in the sun, European frogs prefer to stay calm and out of sight. Giving plenty of hiding spots and maintaining a relaxed, shaded environment will encourage frogs to thrive in your pond.

Lay rocks or flat stones. Add these on the shelves, like retaining walls, around the bottom and sides to hide the liner and provide texture and shelter for frogs. Don't fill in all the areas. Stand some up and lay others down. A helpful tip: Use additional stones or logs to create a visual balance if the ground is uneven, and leave gaps for hiding frogs to use.

Design frog-friendly spaces. Use rocks or stones to create shallow areas, gaps and caves. Frogs love shaded hiding spots, so arrange larger stones for shade and shelter.

Add natural elements. Install deadwood or driftwood for climbing spots and perches. Deadwood provides shelter for frogs and doubles as a habitat for other pond wildlife, such as insects.

Add gravel. Lay about a 3 to 5-cm layer of gravel (or substrate) of mixed sizes over the pond shelves and bottoms, like pepper and salt dusting. However, you don't want layers and layers. You can add pebbles to make a beach where sun-loving frogs can bask and quickly enter or exit the water. This is unusual for European frogs, who like to hang out in the shade.

5. Plant Native Aquatic Plants

Creating a thriving ecosystem for frogs starts with selecting the right plants to support your pond's natural balance and provide essential habitats for amphibians. The next chapter will provide more information about the types of pond plants.

Frogs love aquatic plants. Incorporate different marginals and oxygenating plants in shallow areas to create shade, shelter, and oxygenation. These plants are vital for maintaining a healthy pond ecosystem.

Use water garden pouches. These are ideal for securely holding aquatic plants and soil. Plant miniature water lilies or marginals in the provided pouches, placing them strategically on the shelves. This approach prevents soil from dispersing in the water, ensuring a clean and stable planting setup.

Add floating plants. Floating plants or islands reduce algae growth, offer additional shade, and create safe hiding spots for frogs. Plating plant balls or mini islands is an excellent option for smaller micro ponds. Want to make your own? Watch my step-by-step YouTube guide on crafting these fun and functional features at https://waterfeature.shop/floating-plant-ball.

Simplify your planting process. Using a beginner pond kit ensures that every component is compatible and sized correctly, saving you from the guesswork and potential challenges of mismatched materials. It's like having a blueprint for success in your hands.

6. Fill the Pond with Water

Your pond is almost ready!

Fill slowly. Start with half rainwater and half tap water. Dechlorinate the tap water by adding a Pond Detoxifier to protect the wildlife. If you don't have rainwater, using all tap water is okay. However, I'm not fond of all rainwater due to algae's soft water and lower pH. Pro tip: If unsure about the water level, let the pond settle overnight. This ensures you avoid overfilling and disturbing the setup. You don't need to install an overflow on a small pond as it will not catch much rainwater. But it's always a good idea to know where the level should be to fill to this point. If the low edge is on soil, not stepping on this area or wet ground will only take the soil away, lowering the pond level over time.

Once the pond is complete, add pond treatments. One or several Multi Aqua Sachets will introduce beneficial bacteria, and Multi Clear will keep algae at bay. These treatments help ensure the pond remains clear and algae-free while promoting beneficial bacteria.

Cut back the edges. It is now time to cut off the liner and matting. Please note safety precautions when using sharp tools like knives or scissors, especially when children are helping out. Leave about 15 to 20 cm (6 into 8 in) for liner tucking or overlap to account for any settling and a free board (splash zone of 7 cm).

Use several ways to cover the black liner. Don't roll up, but fold, and don't have the pond matting on top of the liner, touch the soil or be above the water level, as it will pull out the water with capillary action.

7. Let the Pond Settle

Before adding frogs or tadpoles, let the pond settle for a few days. This will allow the water to clear and the environment to stabilise. Remember not to move frogs or tadpoles from long distances to avoid spreading diseases. Below are specific tips for frog ponds.

Skim leaves and debris from the pond's surface in the autumn. Too many decaying leaves can release gases into the pond when covered by ice. Tip: To make this process easier, Consider installing a pond cover net. This net can catch falling leaves and debris, significantly reducing the cleaning you'll need later.

Avoid disturbing hibernating frogs. As temperatures drop, frogs begin hibernating. It's important to avoid disturbing them during this vulnerable time, as this can stress the animals and disrupt their natural cycle.

Instead, allow the frogs to remain undisturbed until the weather warms up again in spring.

Keep an area ice-free with a small aerator or a hot pan. For more detailed methods, consider checking out my winter videos that provide practical demonstrations on maintaining ice-free sections.

Following these guidelines can help create a safe and healthy environment for frogs in your pond.

Beginner's Guide to Building a Vibrant Fish Pond

This guide aims to assist you in creating an attractive, low-maintenance fish pond. Imagine a tranquil garden oasis filled with clear freshwater, lush aquatic plants and happy fish – all without the hassle of complex construction techniques or unsightly equipment above and below the surface.

Whether you're new to pond building or want a straightforward approach, this guide simplifies the process. You can create a stunning aquatic environment using a single pond liner with two protective matting layers and an essential pump and filter system. The goal is to achieve a visually pleasing and functional pond without exposing unsightly black plastic or bulky filter boxes.

A vibrant fish pond kit can also simplify the experience. A fish pond kit is more than just a collection of parts – it's a step towards a worry-free installation. By eliminating trial and error, these kits allow you to focus on the fun of pond building and creating a vibrant environment for your garden.

Use this checklist to gather the essential tools, materials and equipment for a smooth installation.

Materials

- Protective matting: Enough matting is needed to cover the pond liner under and over.
- Flexible pond liner: Everything goes inside the pond liner (I refer to this as the waterproof bag) except the first layer of protective matting that protects the underside.
- Eco pond pump: This submersible pond pump circulates the pond water to the filter (see your pond kit for recommended flow rates).
- Rock pool filter: A rock pool filter provides the filtration for a clean and healthy pond.
- Flexible hose: Water can flow from one side of the pond to another.
- Mesh basket or net: A simple collection basket or net to gather leaves and floating debris
- Waterfall foam: To direct the flowing water
- Aquatic safe substrate: Aquatic soil, flat rocks, stones, gravel and pebbles to provide texture

- Water garden pouches: To contain aquatic plants and keep soil from washing away
- Aquatic plants: Hardy and native aquatic plants, such as miniature water lilies and marginals
- Bottle of pond detoxifier: This product neutralises chlorine and other chemicals in tap water, making it safe for fish.
- Multi aqua sachets: This introduces beneficial bacteria for a healthy pond ecosystem.
- Multi clear: Helps prevent early algae growth and keeps the water clear

Tools

- Spade or shovel: For digging the pond and shaping shelves
- Sharp knife or scissors: Cutting the pond liner and protective matting
- Spirit level: To ensure the pond and surrounding area are even
- Tape measure: This is for accurate pond size and depth measurements.
- Wheelbarrow: For transporting soil, gravel, and other materials
- Garden hose: To mark out the pond shape and fill it with water
- Gardening gloves and work boots: These are for protection during the digging and building phases.

Optional Tools

- Pick axe or grafting bar: If the ground is solid or stoney

Extra Elements:

- Driftwood: Creates hiding spots and visual interest for fish
- Submerged Logs or Manufactured Fish Caves: You must offer fish shelter (hiding places when herons are about).
- Stump Covers: To cover electrical outlets
- Lights: 12v underwater lights

Step-by-Step Guide to Building Your Vibrant Fish Pond

Following this guide, you can confidently create a small, vibrant fish pond that's easy to set up and maintain. This pond design prioritises clear water, healthy fish and a beautiful environment with minimal effort, which is perfect for beginners.

1. Mark Out the Pond Area (Preparing the Ground)

Now, put on your gardening gloves and work boots. Let's dive in and make your fish pond dreams a reality!

Before you start digging, double-check that the liner size and other materials match your intended pond dimensions, including a depth of at least 45 cm to 60 cm (18 to 24 in), to ensure a healthy environment for your fish. If you're working with a pond kit, this process is much easier.

Clear the area. Remove any plants or debris. Save desirable plants for later, and protect or move anything that might get damaged, such as garden furniture.

Mark out the shape. A garden hose outlines the pond's shape. Choose from various shapes (refer to the Planning Your Pond chapter for suggestions). Measure dimensions to confirm they fit your pond kit's requirements.

Check the ground level. Use a spirit level to ensure the area is flat and level. Adjust as needed. Consider creating a terrace if building on a slope. Use a pick axe or a grafting bar if the soil is difficult to dig. If you need to adjust a little, use extra stones and logs to create small retaining walls. Handle large stones safely (get help with anything above 25 kg). You will be surprised by the weight of root balls. If the site or construction area is rough, be extra careful.

2. Excavate the Pond (Digging)

Once the ground levels are established, identify the lowest point and begin digging to the proper depth to maintain a healthy fish environment. This will ensure that your pond has a suitable balance between shallow and deep areas.

Digging depth. Excavate the pond to a depth of the kit, typically 45 cm or 60 cm (18 in to 24 in). This depth provides ample space for your pond fish to swim comfortably.

Create shelves and ledges. Dig four shelves at different levels to create safe, natural hiding spots in the rocks. They also make it easy to arrange water plants, not forgetting it reduces the amount of soil to be removed and time digging.

For the first shelf, the water depth should be at least 15 to 20 cm, with an additional 7 to 10 cm of waterline buffer (pros call this the freeboard) above the surface to prevent overflow, pond fish from jumping out and low edges. Leave enough space for the rock pool filter and the skim cove on the two opposite sides for a longer distance for sweeping the water surface.

After digging down and shovelling out the loose soil on the first level, you can start marking out the next shelf. Go down another 15 to 20 cm below the first shelf, giving a water depth of 40 cm.

Finally, the third shelf should be another 15 to 20 cm down. Depending on the number specified by your pond kit, your pond will typically reach a total depth of 45 or 60 cm.

Shape the pond. Clean and shape the pond as you dig. If you're digging in the sand or the soil is very loose, avoid standing on the edges; if you can't shape the ground as it's too loose, over-dig and backfill as you build the internal walls with stone. Don't put garden soil back inside the waterproof bag. This goes on the outside; you can usually keep the shape without over-digging. Add vertical edges where necessary to help support rocks. Create deeper areas for fish to swim and shelter. You only need upright walls down to 60 cm if you plan on building an internal retaining wall on the inside of the liner. You can get creative with the fish cave and skim cove areas.

Create a skim cove. Position a skim cove anywhere, but ideally on the longest and opposite side of the rock pool filter. It should be easily accessible but not suitable in the centre of your viewing spot. Having 15 to 20 cm of water above the pump will prevent air from getting sucked into the pump, allowing you to also net or rake out leaves.

Dig out a sump area within the first shelf for the pump. The top of the pump should be positioned below the base of the first shelf. Dig out an additional 5 cm all around so the pump fits easily and can be removed easily. This serves as an intake area to keep the pond surface clean.

Be mindful of the hole's location, as it can be a blind hazard once covered until you start building the skim wall. You can over-dig this area, but leave space around the pond's edge to stand rocks up so they are not directly on the pump. Otherwise, you must remove them whenever you want to clean the pump.

Compact for filter. Now that the area for the pump inside the skim cove has been dug out, you want to level a film area opposite the skim cove mouth for the rock pool filter to stand on.

Double-check the depth. Make sure you have excavated the pond to the right depth of 45 cm or 60 cm (18 to 24 in) to provide enough space for fish to swim comfortably. Also, remember the waterline buffer (or freeboard).

Smooth the ground surface. Ensure the pond base and sides are smooth, with no sharp rocks or roots that could puncture the liner. If the ground is dry, use a bloom to brush up any loose soil. If it is crazy wet, scoop out the worst and add protective matting to stop the sloppiness.

Beginner tips for digging. Measure the depth of your spade blade to guide your excavation. It might be 27 or 30 cm, ideal for the first shelf. I have used tape or paint on the blade in the past.

Be careful not to step on the soil you're removing to avoid compacting it further. Work in a line and avoid standing on any dug soil until you have a flat base or a virgin soil shelf to get a better angle for shovelling the loose soil. You don't want to re-compact the soil being removed. To avoid compaction or obstruction, take out chunks of soil and place them in a wheelbarrow or final resting place.

3. Install the Protective Matting and Liner (Waterproofing)

Add the first protective layer. Lay the protective matting over the entire pond excavation. Ensure it fits snugly without gaps. Years ago, we used other less effective methods. We used old newspapers and carpets, but that was no good, as the gases from the carpets were bad for the ground, and the newspaper would get eaten by worms.

Install the pond liner. Place the pond liner over the protective matting, leaving some excess around the pond's edges. Allow the liner to settle for 15 to 20 minutes to adjust to the shape. This layer creates a watertight seal and prevents leaks. Make sure you have an overlap around the edge, as you don't want to start building to find you have too much overlap on one side.

Add the second protective layer. Place a second protective matting layer over the liner. This layer will secure the liner and protect it from above. You don't need to do this in one sheet; it is best to do it in sections, as it acts as padding for rocks and plant containers. When filled with aquatic soil or small rocks, use the water garden pouches to help the liner and the protective matting stay in place.

Beginner tip when lining. Check for air gaps under the liner. If air is trapped, the liner may shift when water is added. Smooth out the liner, ensuring it conforms to the shape of the pond. Go around the deepest section first (the base should be flat), use your feet to work around the shape, and then move up onto the next shelf. You can fold, but be careful to only pull in from the top, not moving the layer below; make sure you use vertical folds to keep the pond edge as high as possible.

4. Set Up Circulation With the Rock Pool Filter and Pump

Position the filter and pump inside the pond liner on the first shelf to ensure proper water circulation and aeration.

Connect the flexible hose to the filter. See details on the pond kit or the filter you're using.

Position the rock pool filter. Place it at the pond's edge, leaving a little space so that if it overflows, the water will return to the pond. Build up around the filter with rocks and blend it in, ensuring water flows back naturally into the pond. Secure it on a sturdy surface and add rocks and plants around it.

Run the pipe. Lay it around the top shelf inside the pond to the skim cove area. Add some rocks or the filled water garden pouches; if you don't, it will have a mind of its own. We will hide the whole hose and even the pump for a natural look.

Beginner tip for filter. In front of the filter outlet, use a couple of framing rocks or branches (big stones or driftwood, which are higher than the top of the filter but not the same size or shape, or they will look like goalposts). This filter provides an elegant, cascading water effect for a much better sound.

5. Install the Skim Cove (Surface Cleaning)

This skim cove is like a harbour with a wall or breaker, so we can control where the pond waste is pulled.

Install the pump. For easy access and maintenance, your pond pump can now be placed in the sump of the skim cove you dug out within the first shelf. Place the pump in the dug-out area, which is on the opposite side of the filter. Lay the pipe down to the pump. Depending on the location of the pump, you might have to cut the pipe.

Connect the pipe. After cutting the flexible hose connected to the filter (if needed), join the pipe to the pump (see the pond kit or the pump you're using). This setup ensures optimal water circulation and keeps the pond water moving, which helps maintain oxygen levels and overall pond health.

Create the skim cove wall. The opening should be opposite the filter for optimal water flow and debris collection. Make sure you leave a gap at the entrance. The size of the opening to the skim cove is specified in the pond kit instructions.

Beginner tip for skim coves. Place a mesh basket or small net in the mouth of the skim cove to collect leaves and debris that get pulled in. This setup helps keep the surface clean and clear of floating matter. Using a skim cove does not stop the use of a leaf net, but it does help keep the surface free of debris.

6. Create Aquatic Art (Designing the Habitat)

Lay rocks and flat stones. Place rocks around each shelf. If it looks good dry, it will look good wet. Always ensure rocks are grounded and stable, leaning backwards into the bank. Lower stones will or might support your next level as you build up. Rock around the plumbing line; you don't want to see anything.

Build fish caves. Use flat stones to create caves and other hiding spots for fish. Avoid placing too many rocks. If you don't want to fill the pond, leave open swimming spaces between the stones so the fish can swim in and out freely.

Add submerged logs or driftwood. Position natural elements for fish to swim around and hide within. Ensure these are securely placed to avoid damaging the liner.

Leave space around the top shelf. Use the aquatic soil for water plant pouches (add these around the higher first shelf).

After the bulk. Spread a mixture of gravel and pebbles thinly around the pond bottom and open areas on any shelves to provide more texture.

Beginner tip for checking for safety. Always check for sharp edges on rocks that might harm fish or puncture the liner. Think about the liner like you would your skin. If you need to ask yourself, "Will the edge of the stone cut my skin unprotected?" The answer is likely "Yes." The same goes for the liner. Be mindful of looking out for sharp edges.

For more tips and samples on aquatic art, you can check out my video on YouTube: https://waterfeature.shop/waterfeatureidea

7. Plant Native Aquatic Plants (Creating an Ecosystem)

Water garden pouches. Place aquatic plants like water lilies and marginals in pouches on the shelves.

Adding other plants. Floating and submerged plants help maintain water clarity and provide shade if needed.

Beginner tip for plants. Watch my YouTube videos for information about the best pond plants and tips on supporting a healthy pond environment by providing shade and oxygenation, which also aids in water clarity. Choose plants that suit the pond size and won't be eaten by the goldfish.

8. Finish the Skim Cove and Filter (Block up the gaps)

So now you have finished all the rock work and built the skim cove walling. On to the next steps.

Seal up the skim cove. It's time to seal the gaps so water can flow where it should. Lift the walling stones and seal or fill in any gaps. The cove doesn't have to be 100% watertight, but the more gaps filled, the better. Sealing the gaps will make the entrance (mouth) more effective.

Seal up the waterfall. If the gaps between the rocks are not sealed, the water coming out of the filter will only exit out of sight. You want to see and hear the water falling or rolling on top of the rocks. Use gravel or rolled-up matting for significant gaps, then add the waterfall foam over the top.

Beginner tip on foam. Watch my video on using waterfall foam or read the instructions, as the instructions can differ depending on which foam you're using. https://waterfeature.shop/waterfallfoam

9. Fill the Pond with Water (Final Steps)

Wash all surfaces. Clean the rocks, gravel and shelves to remove dust and dirt. Pump out or bail out the discoloured water (and repeat as needed). Be careful not to wash out the aquatic soil from the water garden poaches. This process is a must to remove any significant amounts of dust or debris in the gravel and pebbles. Once you're satisfied, pump out the discoloured wastewater.

Fill slowly. Once everything is in place and clean, it's time to fill the pond and prepare it for fish. Fill it slowly with water, not dislodging anything. If using tap or city water, add a Pond Detoxifier to neutralise harmful chemicals. If using rainwater, be mindful of algae growth – up to 50% rainwater is ideal for a balanced pond ecosystem.

Pond treatments. Add the Multi Aqua Sachets as instructed; this introduces beneficial bacteria. Mix up and apply the Multi Clear to keep the water clear of blanket weed.

Cut back the edges. It is now time to cut off the liner and matting. Please note safety precautions when using sharp tools like knives or scissors, especially when children are helping out. Leave about 15 to 20 cm (6 to 8 in) for liner tucking or overlap to account for any settling and a free board (a splash zone of 7cm).

Use several ways to cover the black liner. Don't roll up, but fold, and don't have the pond matting on top of the liner, touch the soil or be above the water level, as it will pull out the water with capillary action.

10. Let the Pond Settle (Final Preparations)

Wait. Allow the pond to stabilise for a few days before introducing fish. Check water quality parameters to ensure a safe environment for your fish (see the pond care chapter for more information).

Enjoy your pond. Sit back and enjoy your pond. For the first couple of days, it might not be as ideal without fish, but enjoy the sound and ripples you have created.

Beginner tip for establishing a healthy pond. If you can access mature filter media or a bucket full of mature gravel from another garden pond, use it to accelerate the ecosystem's development. As these will be alive, transport them damp and not in water. Don't dry or allow strong sunlight to kill off the rocks. Don't just take stuff from the wild, as you might bring in pests and viruses.

Beginner's Guide to Constructing an Elegant Water Garden

Transform your garden with a stunning, formal, small water garden using simple construction methods and a unique raised design. In this guide, we'll show you how to create a striking, functional and beautiful water garden, even if you're new to pond building.

This guide aims to assist beginners in creating and constructing an elegant water garden using a straightforward method that even beginners can master. Imagine a formal, rectangular pond outlined with rustic garden timbers, filled with vibrant water plants and reflective black-dyed water to create a dramatic effect, store the heat from the sun and show off the flowers.

This water garden will be partly in-ground and partly raised, perfect for creating a defined focal point in your garden. With clear steps and practical advice, I'll show you how to build a pond that looks professional and is manageable for a beginner with some basic DIY skills.

This guide assumes you're working with a complete pond kit that includes timbers for the frame and brackets for stability. If not, here is a guide on what you'll need.

Materials

- Timbers: Your wooden frame requires four complete courses of wood. The timbers are laid flat, and each timber measures 1.2 m by 20 cm by 10 cm for our single-person installation.
- Metal brackets: Secure the corners with heavy-duty internal and external brackets.
- Protective matting: Enough to cover both under and over the pond liner
- Flexible pond liner: The liner must be big enough to fit the pond's internal dimensions and account for the depth and side walls.
- Composite deck boards: These secure the liner, matting at the top and covering any exposed areas.

- Drainage panels: These are used to protect the pond base from heavy plant pots and water gardeners who are getting into the business of caring for plants.
- Water garden pouches: Pre-filled with aquatic soil for planting
- Aquatic soil: Suitable for water lilies and marginals
- Black pond dye: To prevent algae and give the pond a reflective surface
- Pond-safe fertiliser tablets: These are used to encourage full plant development.

Tools

- Spade or shovel: For digging the pond and shaping shelves
- Sharp knife or scissors: Cutting the pond liner and protective matting
- Spirit level: To ensure the pond and surrounding area are even
- Tape measure: This is for accurate pond size and depth measurements
- Wheelbarrow: For transporting soil, gravel, and other materials
- Mains power electric screwdriver: To screw in the timber locks into the timbers
- Gardening gloves: These are for protection during the digging and moving the timbers around.
- Waterproof waders: For getting in the pond place the plants and keep you dry

Optional Tools

- Mitre saw: For cutting your (uncut) timbers (just use the pond kits if you don't have the experience)
- Small hand saw: Cutting deck boards or other timbers

Step-by-Step Guide to Building Your Elegant Water Garden

1. Set Up the Framework (Creating the Pond Shape)

Remember to wear appropriate safety gear and ensure a safe working environment when handling heavy materials like timbers and brackets.

Place and build the timber frame. Start by laying the base timbers in a rectangle. Choose or create a flat area in your garden for a neat appearance. Ensure each layer of timbers is level to avoid a lopsided pond. The timbers need to be flat to hold the weight of the water.

Now, find the lowest spot and dig in the rest of the base timbers to that level unless you plan to raise the garden levels. If this is the case, use concrete or my preferred sub-base of crushed hardcore with a membrane under this base material. Before securing, double-check each corner for square alignment using a tape measure or corner bracket.

Ensure each layer is flat and level before adding the next. The framework timbers should be around four levels high. If you are not using our kit, you create an external height of 40 cm.

A common mistake to avoid is not spending enough time on the first complete layer. Starting with an uneven first timber layer will only cause problems later.

Reinforce the frame. Connect the corners using the metal brackets on the inside and the external metal brackets for extra strength (see your pond kit for the amount supplied). Add extra brackets or screws if necessary to create any steps or tie in the pond into the landscape and keep the timbers secure to prevent shifting over time. Use an electric screwdriver to secure the brackets in place.

After constructing the frame, check all corners and joints for stability.

Pro tip. If you want a more polished look and are confident about a tighter joint, consider a mitred cut and mitring all the corners of the timbers.

2. Excavate the Pond (Creating the Depth)

Digging the pond. Inside the timber frame, dig out the middle section to another depth of 30 cm (in addition to the 40 cm internal depth of the timbers). This will create a total water depth of 60 cm with 10 cm of waterline buffer (freeboard). You are making a semi-raised pond with a maximum internal depth of 70 cm.

Ensure the sides and bottom are even, leaving a flat surface in the centre for the water lilies and other deep-water plants. The size of this area depends on what plants you want to grow. I dig close to the front edge as I only sometimes want plants in the foreground of the water plant display. You can choose if you want more water lilies than marginals. If using the drainage panels to protect the base, I recommend using these to mark out the area you want to dig, giving the side wall an angle. Hence, they are not straight down, or you will need to retain these edges with internal concrete blocks (again laid flat or using hollow 9-inch wide ones).

Compact the soil gently to create a stable base. Use a spirit level to check that the base is even and that the sides of the hole align with the timber frame. Also, ensure that there are no voids around the base of the timbers, which need to support the top section of the pond water.

3. Install the Protective Matting and Liner (Waterproofing)

Lay the first protective layer. Once satisfied, lay the first layer of protective matting on the ground inside the pond. Position the protective matting inside the pond, covering the entire excavation and the sides of the timber walls. Smooth it out and ensure no air gaps or loads of creases.

Place the pond liner. Now, place the flexible pond liner over the protective matting, leaving enough excess around the edges to overlap with the timber frame.

Allow the liner to settle for 15 to 20 minutes, adjusting it to fit snugly into the pond's contours.

Pro tip. Press the matting and liner smoothly into place using a clean broom. This will prevent you from getting on your hands and knees.

Add the second layer of protective matting. To prevent damage from the plant containers, lay the second layer over the liner, especially on the base and sides.

Install the drainage panels. Clip the panels together to create a single sheet and install it on top of the protective matting at the base. You do not need them on the top shelf.

4. Secure the Liner and Finish the Top of the Pond (Creating a Professional Look)

Add water to check the liner's position. Fill the pond above the first top shelf to ensure the liner is tucked neatly. Put on your waterproof boots, get in, and fold the liner so no parts are exposed above the composite boards.

Fix the composite deck boards. Use the composite deck boards to cover the liner's top. Place one board inside the pond to descend into the water (once full of pond water), screw the board into place with the brackets and use the top two boards horizontally. These cover the top edge to hide exposed liner ends and provide a clean, polished finish. These boards hold the liner in place securely. If you're not using our kit, use a power drill to pre-drill holes in the composite boards before screwing them in to prevent splitting. Use patches or seam tape to create a thicker pond liner edge where you're going through the liner; this avoids tears later down the line.

Always cover the liner edges to prevent damage and keep the pond tidy. Don't cover the liner with protective matting above the vertical sides; this might wick out the water.

5. Add Water and Planting Soil (Preparing the Plant Zones)

Water garden pouches. Place water garden pouches filled with aquatic soil on the first shelf. These pouches can accommodate marginals and are perfect for smaller plants. You can double stack or use other items (bricks or blocks) under smaller plants. Ensure all plants are spaced to allow full development and avoid crowding.

Plant water lilies in the deeper areas of your pond to enhance beauty and provide shade for aquatic life. Position them on the edge of pre-filled water garden pouches to ensure healthy growth and stability. For best results, place lilies directly at the pond's bottom, around 60 cm below the waterline. If you're starting with smaller plants, use bricks or blocks to raise them gradually. Space your lilies evenly to allow sunlight to reach all leaves and flowers. Need a guide? Watch my step-by-step video on how to re-pot water lilies at https://waterfeature.shop/re-potting-water-lilies.

Continue filling the pond with water. Slowly fill the pond to the correct level. The shelf will hold your deep-water marginals. Use a gentle flow to avoid dislodging soil or fertiliser from the plant pouches.

6. Apply Black Pond Dye (Enhancing Aesthetics)

Dye application. Follow the product's instructions to apply the black pond dye safely. Start with half the recommended dosage and gradually increase until the desired effect is achieved. Avoid using too much dye initially, as it can darken the water more than intended and is challenging to dilute (you will have to do water changes or wait for the sun to weaken the dye).

The black dye will suppress algae growth, attract sun heat, disguise all the bricks and blocks, and create a dramatic reflective surface, giving your pond a professional, formal appearance.

Submerged plants are not recommended for use with black dye as they won't get enough light. However, you can omit the dye and introduce submerged oxygenating plants for a different effect.

7. Enjoy Your Water Garden!

Sit back and admire your new elegant water garden. The reflective black water and vibrant plant life will attract attention and provide a beautiful, low-maintenance feature to your garden.

Every ripple and reflection you see will remind you of your hard work and dedication to building something exceptional.

Final Thoughts

Congratulations on reaching the end of this chapter! Whether you've followed the steps to create a serene frog pond, a vibrant fish pond or an elegant water garden, you've taken the first steps towards becoming a true pond enthusiast. Each of these projects, while varied in their focus and style, embodies the beauty, tranquillity and life that only a garden water feature can bring. I hope these step-by-step guides have inspired you to embrace the art of pond building with confidence and enthusiasm.

I'd love to see how your project turned out! Please share your pond-building journey and post pictures in my "Ponds and Water Gardening" group on Facebook. It's a fantastic place to connect with fellow pond lovers, exchange ideas and showcase your new aquatic masterpiece.

As you reflect on the steps outlined in this chapter, you'll notice how planning, preparation and the right tools make all the difference. A beginner pond kit is designed with these principles in mind, making it the perfect starting point for first-time builders.

Beginner pond kits are crafted to simplify the process of planning and installation. With every element pre-selected for compatibility and durability, these kits ensure a seamless start to your pond-building adventure.

They take the stress out of measuring, sourcing, and matching components, giving you the confidence to build a functional and beautiful pond. With a beginner pond kit, you're setting yourself up for success while avoiding many common DIY pitfalls.

Want a visual guide to help with your pond installation? Check out our step-by-step video tutorials at https://waterfeature.shop/step-by-step-installations and easily follow along.

Chapter 6
TIPS FOR SELECTING POND PLANTS AND AQUATIC LIFE

Starting a pond can feel overwhelming. What if you choose the wrong plants, struggle with maintenance or fail to create a balanced habitat? Don't worry – this chapter will show you simple, beginner-friendly strategies to avoid common mistakes, select the right plants and build a thriving ecosystem. Let's take the first step towards a beautiful, low-maintenance pond you'll love.

A Beginner's Guide to Pond Plants

Right off the bat, allow me to offer two tips. First, start with hardy plants. These are beginner-friendly and can survive in different conditions, giving you an excellent chance to learn and build confidence before moving on to more delicate species. Second, be sure to balance plant types.

It is essential to include a mix of floating, submerged and marginal plants. Each type has a role: Floating plants shade the water, submerged plants add oxygen and marginal plants help filter and clean the water. A balanced mix will create a healthy environment for fish and other pond creatures.

Creating a garden pond is a fun and exciting project. Choosing the right plants is crucial to keeping your pond looking great and healthy. Pond plants make your pond pretty, help clean the water, provide shade and provide homes for animals like frogs and fish. Even if you know little about water gardening, this guide will help you pick the best plants and learn where to put them in your pond.

Why Choosing the Right Plants Is Important for Your Pond

They will help your pond look pretty. Adding a few plants can enrich the habitat, offering aquatic animals places to explore and hide when needed. While artificial decorations can serve this purpose, live plants create a more dynamic and vibrant environment. Plants like water lilies have beautiful flowers that look like fireworks on the water's surface.

They will help the water stay clean. Some plants, like hornwort, release oxygen into the water. I call this "pearling," as you can see the oxygen coming off in tiny air bubbles that look like pearls. They also absorb nutrients that algae (the green stuff) need to grow, so they help keep the water clear.

They give shade. Plants can help control algae growth by blocking sunlight, as the green stuff can still flourish despite a good filter. Some plants, like water lilies, also provide shade, which cools the water and gives fish a place to hide from birds.

If you choose plants that do different jobs, you can make your pond a happy, healthy and beautiful place for fish and other wildlife.

The Various Types of Pond Plants and How They Work

Pond plants come in different types depending on where they grow in or around the water. Here's a look at the various kinds and how they can help your pond.

1. Moisture-loving plants (Like Someone Standing in a Puddle or a Wet Field)

These plants don't grow in the water but love the wet, muddy ground around the pond, like someone who likes standing in a puddle (see the figure on page 135, left-hand side marked "1"). They like to keep their feet wet but don't want to be completely underwater.

- **Blue Siberian Iris** (*Iris sibirica*). This plant blooms with beautiful purple flowers and grows well in the damp soil around the pond. It adds lots of color and is easy to grow.
- **Red Cardinal Flower** (*Lobelia cardinalis*). This impressive plant, with bright red flowers, grows in the moist soil around ponds.

2. Marginal Plants (Like Someone Standing in a Pond with Rubber Boots)

Marginal plants grow at the edges of ponds with their roots underwater, but most of the foliage above water is like someone standing in a pond with rubber boots. They love getting their roots wet but don't want to be entirely underwater (See the figure on page 135 for both the marked spots "2").

- **Marsh Marigold** (*Caltha palustris*). This plant has bright yellow flowers and grows in shallow water at the pond's edge. It's great for spring and attracts bees and butterflies.
- **Pickerel Weed** (*Pontederia cordata*). It has blue flowers and grows in deeper water along the edges, like wearing "thigh waders" and water that goes up to your knees. This combination is perfect for bringing colour and attracting insects.

3. Floating Plants (Like Someone Relaxing on a Li-lo)

Floating plants are great for beginners because they are easy to look after. They float on the top of the water with their roots hanging down, just like someone floating on a li-lo (a pool float). You don't have to plant them – just place them in or on the pond water (in the middle of the figure on page 135, we have five floating plants marked "3")!

- **Water Lettuce** (*Pistia stratiotes*). This plant looks like a green, fluffy rosette that floats on the water. It helps keep the pond cool and can prevent algae by blocking sunlight.
- **Watercress** (*Nasturtium aquaticum*). You can even buy a bag of watercress from the supermarket and pop it in your pond. It loves cold water and helps clean up extra nutrients in the pond.

4. Submerged Plants (Like Someone Snorkeling Underwater)

These plants (in the middle bottom of the figure on page 135, and on the right marked "4") grow entirely underwater, like someone snorkelling. They help keep the pond healthy by releasing oxygen and providing hiding places for fish.

- **Hornwort** (*Ceratophyllum demersum*). It is an excellent beginner plant with feathery leaves that lives underwater. It makes oxygen and helps keep the water clear.
- **Mare's Tail** (*Hippuris vulgaris*). This plant multiplies through its roots and has bottlebrush stems that rise from the pond water. It absorbs excess nutrients that algae need, helping to keep your pond water clean and safe for fish.

Waterlilies

The water lily is a unique plant because it grows with its roots and rhizomes anchored in a substrate under the water (like the submerged plants at 4. on page 135). Its leaves need to be on the surface so they can breathe in and out, like a paddleboard. Water lilies will give you beautiful flowers with enough sun and plant food. Depending on the variety, some can grow in very shallow water (around 10 cm / 4" above the substrate), while others like deeper spots (say 90 cm / 3', but I have seen them much deeper).

They provide shade, so they help reduce algae growth and create a stunning focal point in any pond. These plants don't like constant water hitting the leaves (rain will flow or run off the leaves). If the leaves grow up out of the water, it's a sign the water lilies are too shallow so move them deeper or replace them with small varieties.

- **Mini Water Lily** (*Nymphaea pygmaea helvola*) is a true miniature waterlily producing delicate yellow blooms. Although I have seen it grow in 45 cm (18") of water in warmer climates with extra care and feeding, I mainly grow and recommend around 25 cm (10") of water above the crowns here in the UK.
- **My Favourite Water Lily** (*Nymphaea laydekeri fulgens*) is vibrant Burgundy-Red, a fantastic choice for beginners with small and patio ponds. This variety stays compact and flowers freely for long periods. Its deep red blooms make it a striking addition to any pond while still being manageable in size.

How to Choose the Right Pond Plants

As a side note, I still suggest having plants in your pond, even if you're aiming to create a simple pool. For example, when making a mini swimming pool for goldfish, a robust filtration system might lead you to skip traditional aquatic plants. However, incorporating plants offers several advantages, even in a fish-centric setup. They can increase the fish's comfort, promote a healthier ecosystem by controlling algae and regulating temperature and enhance the environment for the fish. If you decide not to include plants, regularly monitoring water conditions to keep the fish healthy is crucial.

Adding a few strategically placed plants can brighten the space and maintain a clean aesthetic, even with a minimalist design.

There are three main things to consider when picking plants for your pond:

1. Where they grow. Some plants need to be underwater, some float and others like to be near the pond's edge or just stand in the water. Make sure you pick plants that fit where you want them to go.

2. How much sunlight is needed. Some plants need a lot of sun, while others thrive in shade. Check the amount of sunlight your pond gets daily to ensure your plants thrive.

3. The size of the pond. Choose smaller plants like water lettuce and marsh marigolds if your pond is small. Larger plants, like pickerel rush or water lilies, can be used in more extensive ponds.

Creating a pond filled with beautiful plants is a great way to turn your garden into a peaceful place to relax and watch nature. As a beginner, start with strong, easy-to-grow plants. They're simple to care for and will help you build confidence. Once you get the hang of it, you can add more plants and make your pond even more special!

Many resources are available to help you make informed choices. Specialist water plant nurseries, conservation organisations and educational platforms offer valuable insights and advice on choosing and caring for pond plants that suit your needs. Local garden centres and aquatic shops can provide hands-on experience and recommendations, though it's crucial to ensure you buy mature, healthy plants. For further guidance, explore my library of over 20 pond plant videos. These videos are packed with expert tips and tutorials to help you select, plant and care for pond plants, ensuring a balanced and vibrant pond ecosystem. Watch them here: https://waterfeature.shop/pond-plants-videos.

A Beginner's Guide to Pond Fish

From Hardy Goldfish to Koi

My grandfather kept a goldfish called Badger in a green water tank beside the dining table. I remember seeing a flash of gold whenever he would feed Badger, of all things, cheese. I also remember there were goldfish kept in a cattle trough close to the farmhouse at my Uncle Bill's. One weekend, my cousins Adrian and Derek were allowed to fish the farm pond at Uncle Bill's, and I remember seeing a photo of Derek with a giant goldfish (well, it turned out to be a golden orfe). These experiences led me to keep fish in goldfish bowls. Some fish even came from the visiting fun fairs where you could win them at games (though they sadly never survived very long in these conditions).

At that age, I could not afford the expensive koi. But I had no complaints. These fantastic little bars of gold are incredibly resilient and require minimal care. Goldfish are also famous for their adaptability to various temperatures, flourishing in cold and warm water! They often breed well in my planted ponds, making them ideal for anyone just starting with a garden pond that wants fish. I remember buying a bag of 30 goldfish when I first built my pond, which is crazy to me now as that pond was only 3 m by 2 m. I recommend up to 12 goldfish nowadays for that size pond. Goldfish made my transition into pond care a breeze. With their vibrant colours and lively personalities, they not only brought life to my pond but also helped me grasp the essentials of pond maintenance without overwhelming me.

As you know, I started with one goldfish pond at my mum's house in 1989. Over the years, I added more, eventually establishing three different systems with two large DIY filters.

This journey introduced me to koi. One of our neighbours, Les Welsh, had a vast Japanese koi pool, complete with a tea house in one of the neighbouring gardens. I would spend hours learning, talking to him after school and going to koi shops and shows. As you can tell, I quickly became passionate about koi.

However, keeping koi isn't for beginners. They require a pond at least 5 m by 3 m large and a meter deep. These fish grow fast in the first 5 years, potentially reaching over 1 m long (36 in). You need ample space and efficient filtration to keep the water quality high.

Over the years, I have talked to many people about keeping koi. The best way for me to explain these creatures is by comparing them to fully grown cats, all kept in a single room. Let's say the room is the size of the pond, and the koi are the same weight as the cats (often more, really). If, for example, we were to place six cats in a single room, no doubt it would quickly become a mess. Cats and koi need much more work than goldfish. For comparison, goldfish will only grow to around 25 cm (10 in).

My Local Pet Shop

When I built my first few ponds, I was excited to fill them with fish. Like the adults I work with now, I also wanted many different kinds of fish. I remember that, with any chance I could get, I'd go to the local pet shop in my hometown and marvel at all the colourful tropical fish in the aquariums. I was told they were hard to keep, and my dad had even killed a few and given up before I had a chance to learn from this setup. Tropical fish are not all hard to keep; coldwater pond fish are much more manageable in most cases.

I would stand and stare at the three coldwater fibreglass tanks full of goldfish, big koi and other exotic cold water species. I was so eager to recreate these types of setups that the shop had, but I didn't realise how tricky it could be to manage different kinds of fish, not to mention when they all come from various sources. At the time, I didn't know much about biosecurity or the importance of quarantine when introducing new fish, and I ended up learning the hard way. I'd buy fish from various places and mix them, only to see them struggle or even die because of diseases and stress.

You can have loads of fish. The shopkeeper would say, "They stay small." This information is correct but misleading, and there are better ways of thinking nowadays. Small zoos were common when I was growing up, so keeping animals in small cages wasn't unusual. The world has changed for the better. We still have a long way to go in water gardening and fish keeping, but more educated people are now teaching.

However, back in the day, I would be sold koi and other fish for indoor aquariums and different setups. Plus, I read how the Japanese – the leading experts, of course – kept koi in small concrete pools over winter, but now I know this is the same as bringing cattle to the shed and back out. They don't stay there all year. They enter the fields in the spring, and the Japanese fish enter the mud ponds. The Japanese also change lots of water and add salt to the winter fish houses.

So, where was this information coming from?

Goldfish and koi release hormones into the pond water to stop them from growing. If you are not changing the water and the pond is a closed system, meaning there is no inlet or outlet, it is assumed that they will stay small. But does that mean it is now acceptable to buy loads of small fish as the hormones will accumulate, supposedly limiting the fish's growth?

How wrong could we be?

When my DIY filters leaked, **my fish grew**.

When I left the hose on, **my fish grew**.

When my pond had excellent conditions, **my fish grew**.

So when my fish outgrew their tanks, I'd move them to the pond, thinking I was giving them more space. But soon enough, they would get too big even for the pond, and I'd have to find new homes for them.

Through these experiences, I realised that keeping things simple is the best way to start with fish in a pond.

How to Choose Fish for Your Pond Without Overcomplications

Buy Fish from One Supplier

Purchase your fish from a trusted supplier and get them all in one go. This reduces the risk of introducing diseases and ensures that your fish come from the same system, making it easier for them to adjust to your pond environment.

Avoid Mixing Pond and Tank Fish

Mixing species can be challenging, as some fish need help with temperature fluctuations and water conditions, leading to losses. Like fancy goldfish, coldwater tank fish often don't thrive in ponds without stable temperatures.

It's best to separate tank and pond species to avoid stress and overcrowding.

For example, I have always wanted a bubble-eyed goldfish pond, but I got bored of it in an aquarium, so what would be different about an indoor pond? They can't mix with other goldfish as they get damaged when combined with other fish during feeding.

Think About Growth

Even goldfish can grow quite large in a pond. Make sure your pond has enough space for the fish to grow, and plan for the future

by researching the adult size of the species you choose. For example, I loved golden orfes for their bright orange and carrot-like appearance, like the one my cousin caught fishing from the farm pond. These guys remain active throughout the winter and have a feeding habit similar to trout's. As a kid, I bought them for my fish pond, but they always jumped out. Later, I learned they wanted a medium to large pond (at least 5 m by 3 m).

Quarantine New Additions

You must have a quarantine setup to add new fish from different sources. Quarantining new fish for a few weeks before adding them to the pond helps prevent the spread of diseases. I always had problems moving fish around or adding new fish to others. Avoid taking fish from friends if you don't have quarantine facilities; free fish might be attractive, but how would you feel if your fish were to suffer?

By keeping things simple and planning carefully, you can enjoy a healthy, thriving pond without the stress and heartbreak of losing fish. Remember, starting small and learning as you go is the best approach to building your confidence and creating a beautiful fish pond that you can enjoy for years. For expert advice, check out my pond fish videos here: https://waterfeature.shop/pond-fish-videos.

A Beginner's Guide to Aquatic Wildlife

If you inherit a pond that was previously a koi pond and no longer has fish, you can adapt it into a thriving wildlife habitat. Instead of focusing on building a new pond, you should assess what you already have and make simple modifications to attract local aquatic wildlife effectively. Here are some tips.

Understand your local ecosystem. Research the species native to your area. Not all wildlife can be attracted everywhere. Plants like red cardinal flowers may draw hummingbirds in the US but won't attract them to the UK. Similarly, specific dragonfly species may not be present in all regions, so tailor your approach to attract natural wildlife.

Adapt the pond's structure. If the pond lacks shallow areas due to its previous use for koi, transform these spaces by adding floating islands or installing structures like an Aqua Blox (plastic drainage crates). These crates provide shallow and safe areas for amphibians, like frogs and newts, to access and lay eggs and spots for birds to drink and bathe.

Incorporate natural features. Add rocks, logs and plants around the edges and within the pond itself. These features create hiding places and basking spots for amphibians and insects, mimicking natural habitats without drastically altering your existing pond.

Introduce native plants. Use plants native to your region, such as oxygenating plants like hornwort or marginal plants like irises. Native plants attract local species and create a balanced ecosystem, ensuring the pond supports wildlife naturally found in the area. Avoid introducing non-native species as they may not suit the environment or could become invasive.

Avoid taking wildlife from natural waterways. Removing animals, plants or fish from natural water bodies is illegal in many places. Instead, attract wildlife by creating the right conditions in your pond. For example, you could ask friends for tadpoles during early spring – tadpoles will help control algae and grow into frogs that aid in pest control.

Minimise chemical use. Do not use chemical treatments for algae or pests; they can harm or deter wildlife. Instead, let the natural inhabitants, such as frogs and dragonflies, manage pest populations and keep the ecosystem balanced.

Creating a wildlife-friendly pond allows you to enjoy a thriving ecosystem while supporting local biodiversity. With the right approach, you can attract frogs, birds, and beneficial insects to your garden, all while maintaining a low-maintenance, eco-friendly pond.

Watch my wildlife pond videos here: https://waterfeature.shop/wildlife-pond-videos for expert tips and inspiration.

A Recap: How to Introduce Life to Your Pond

Creating a thriving garden pond involves more than just adding water; it requires nurturing plants, carefully introducing aquatic life (including fish, if you want to keep them), and creating conditions to attract wildlife while ensuring safety. Each element transforms your pond into a balanced and sustainable habitat.

Plants

Start with hardy aquatic plants like water lilies and oxygenators, which provide shade, improve water quality, create habitats for insects and fish and support a balanced ecosystem. You can buy them from water garden centres or rehome them from friends' ponds.

Avoid transferring invasive weeds like blanket weed or duckweed from other ponds. When transporting plants, keep them moist – use a sealed container to keep oxygenators damp and shield them from wind and sun. If transporting in bags, cover them to avoid creating a sun trap, especially on hot days.

Fish

Introduce fish gradually, beginning with hardy species like goldfish. Ensure water conditions are stable before adding them. You can buy fish from a store or rehome them from friends' ponds (but remember, biosecurity and quarantine everything new). Transport fish safely using a watertight container with a lid or line a bucket with a strong bin bag to prevent water spillage. When adding fish from a store, float the bag in your pond for at least 15 minutes so the water temperature can equalise, reducing stress and shock.

Aquatic Wildlife

Create varied pond depths, add rocks, and place plants around the edges to attract wildlife. This invites insects, birds and amphibians, helping your pond become a natural, thriving habitat. When the frogs start spawning in early spring, ask your friends if you can have some spawn. Tadpoles help control algae and eventually transform into frogs, aiding pest control.

Ensure the pond has shallow areas for them to thrive or floating islands with lots of foliage so the froglets can hide from the local garden birds.

Six Takeaways for Choosing What to Put in Your Pond

Creating a vibrant pond is a rewarding journey that invites thoughtful planning and a deeper connection to nature. Keep these guiding principles in mind:

Start simple. Begin with resilient plants like marsh marigolds and hornwort, and choose hardy fish such as goldfish or colourful shubunkins. As you gain experience, you can explore larger, more intricate ponds with koi.

Balance your ecosystem. Use a mix of floating, submerged and marginal plants to provide shade, oxygen and a well-balanced habitat. Native plants are especially beneficial for attracting local wildlife.

Plan for growth. Research the potential sizes of your plants and fish to ensure your pond has ample space for them to thrive. Implement quarantine measures for new fish to maintain a healthy, pest-free environment.

Enhance wildlife habitat. Design your pond with shallow areas and natural features like rocks and logs. These not only enhance the habitat but also encourage wildlife to settle in. Avoid chemicals and let nature help maintain balance and manage algae and pests.

Careful introductions. Introduce fish and aquatic animals gradually, ensuring stable water conditions to help them adjust comfortably.

Support native species. Learn about the needs of local wildlife and create an inviting sanctuary that fosters biodiversity.

Now that you're equipped with these principles, you're ready to create a pond that will flourish for years to come.

For expert advice and inspiration, dive into my YouTube playlists on pond plants, fish and eco-friendly ponds. These resources will deepen your understanding and help you enjoy the process of building your aquatic sanctuary.

Chapter 7
KEEPING IT BEAUTIFUL WITH MINIMAL EFFORT

A low-maintenance pond design doesn't mean zero care, but it becomes less demanding than tending a lawn or flower bed with the proper setup. Designing a pond that works with nature creates a balanced ecosystem (where waste is naturally converted into water and carbon dioxide), nourishing plant life and keeping the pond clear.

My Journey to a Self-Sustaining Pond

Over the years, I've evolved my approach to pond design with low maintenance in mind. In 2014, I created my first natural, self-sustaining ecosystem. I was sceptical then; I didn't believe a fish pond could be clear for very long without constant maintenance or a UV clarifier.

I even installed UV clarifiers in the first three ecosystem ponds I built to keep customers' expectations. Interestingly, I never had to turn them on. Two ponds still have the original bulbs; we removed the clarifier after an upgrade for the third.

The shift in design was eye-opening. I limited the number of fish to control the waste load on these systems and chose appropriate adult sizes, ensuring that all the pond's natural processes weren't overwhelmed. With a more extensive filtration system tailored to handle occasional debris, we only needed to clean the filters once annually in the spring (very different from once or twice a week). This approach also fostered a healthier environment where nature did much of the work. It's allowed me and my customers to step back and enjoy the ponds without constant intervention, trusting the new pond design and natural processes to do the heavy lifting.

I used to enjoy flushing my koi filters and watching the waste pour out, but now the natural processes within the pond handle much of this. Yes, we still clean the filter systems, but they are far from the traditional setups I had for twenty-five years prior. This approach has allowed me to fully embrace the water gardening lifestyle at home with multiple ponds – now I have places to savour my coffee in the morning, enjoy lazy lunches near the water on sunny weekends and numerous places to unwind with a beer or cocktail at dusk as all of the ponds thrive around me. The result? Time saved, healthier ecosystems and the lasting beauty of ponds that practically care for themselves.

Essential Maintenance Tasks

With experience, my approach has evolved to using more prominent self-sustaining natural filtration techniques, working with Mother Nature and creating ecosystems. If you don't have one of these systems, you will have more work, but with just a few simple tasks, you can achieve low-maintenance ponds. Mastering these essentials will prevent common issues and make pond care more enjoyable for beginners.

Setting Up a Regular Routine

Creating a regular schedule makes pond care manageable and stress-free. Basic checks, like monitoring water flow, go a long way in keeping your pond healthy.

Filter Cleaning

Weekly cleaning of the mechanical filter and monthly cleaning of the biological filter help maintain good water flow and control algae. If you have a mechanical filter that catches debris, a simple rinse with tap water works since it doesn't rely on bacteria. A biological filter should be rinsed gently with water from the pond itself to preserve the beneficial bacteria that help break down waste.

One client struggled with cloudy water because he aggressively cleaned his filters weekly, washing away the biofilm. Your biological filter doesn't need to be perfectly clean – just damp and out of direct sunlight when cleaning (don't let it dry out, or sunlight burns the bacteria).

Visual Health Checks

Spending time by your pond helps you understand its natural rhythms and spot any early signs of change. Look for unusual fish behaviour, changes in water clarity or other shifts in the pond's appearance. Regularly observing the pond is often more effective than testing the water for specific parameters. Note and monitor if you notice something unusual, like foam on the surface or fish "flashing." If it resolves naturally, all's well; if it worsens, you may need to act.

Many new pond owners rush to chemicals or treatments at the first sign of trouble. Often, a bit of patience and observation are best. Stress can harm fish and other aquatic life, so try not to catch or net them unless necessary. Let them rest in a relaxed environment.

Algae Control

Algae play a role in your pond's ecosystem, but too much can cause issues or indicate an imbalance. Removing visible algae, like blanketweed, with a net or garden cane is often best. Some people use parcel tape to attach toilet brushes to them.

If blanketweed persists, I recommend you try https://waterfeature.shop/multi-clear as a proactive measure to address algae without upsetting the pond's natural harmony.

This eco-friendly treatment is beginner-friendly, helping prevent blanketweed from taking hold and keeping your water clear. It's a great preventive measure that allows your pond's natural balance to stay intact without aggressive chemicals.

Dealing with blanket weed in your pond can be frustrating, but you can effectively control and prevent it with the right approach. For practical solutions and expert advice, watch my step-by-step video guide on how to get rid of blanket weed at https://waterfeature.shop/blanket-weed-treatment.

Clients often worry about green water, but I've seen aquatic life naturally balance it, especially in still-water ponds. Draining all the water is rarely needed; some mature pond water helps maintain the biofilm that clears the water. If green water becomes an issue, try partial water changes, but avoid large-scale changes as they can disrupt the pond's balance.

Surface Skimming

Clearing leaves and debris from the pond's surface keeps the water clear and prevents decay. Removing leaves prevents them from sinking, decomposing, and turning the water murky. If you have a swim cove or skimmer, these collect leaves for easy removal. I recommend this pond cleaning net: https://waterfeature.shop/pond-cleaning-net for routine cleaning. Its design helps you navigate pond edges without damaging them.

Leaving leaves to accumulate in the pond turns it into a teapot, or in other words, "tea-stained." I recommend regular skimming to keep the water clear and oxygen levels high, especially in the autumn when more debris falls into the pond.

Seasonal Care for Your First Pond

Season	What to Check	Tasks	What to Avoid	Enjoy
Spring	Water clarity, equipment, plants	Remove large debris by hand, add new plants and clean filters	Overfeeding the life in the pond or disturbing tadpoles	Watching life return to the pond, mating time, fish feeding
Summer	Water levels, oxygen levels	Trim plants, top up water and feed fish	Letting water stagnate or overheat	Thriving plants and flowers, feeding fish and wildlife
Autumn	Leaves and debris entering the water	Net leaves cut back dying plants	Allowing debris to decay in the pond	Preparing for a clean, quiet winter
Winter	Ice-free areas, equipment	Keep part of the surface free from ice	Breaking ice manually or overfeeding fish	A serene low-maintenance pond

Designing a Self-Sustaining Pond

Creating a self-sustaining ecosystem is the best way to achieve low-maintenance pond care. Using natural filtration and maintaining ecological balance minimises the need for frequent maintenance. The entire system acts as a filter in these ponds, creating a self-cleaning effect.

Ecosystem ponds typically use a skimmer and a waterfall filter. Beneficial bacteria thrive on surface areas like rocks, gravel and plastic filter media, helping convert ammonia and nitrites (which can hurt fish and other aquatic life if there are too many) into less harmful elements. To preserve bacterial colonies, avoid thoroughly cleaning these areas and rinse solids from biofilters with pond water only.

Natural Filtration Techniques

Plant-Based Filtration

Aquatic plants like water lilies, irises, ornamental reeds, rushes (not the aggressive ones, which can damage rubber pond liners and are not suitable for these situations) and watercress act as natural filters, absorbing excess nutrients and preventing algae blooms. Plants with extensive root systems are especially effective in balancing the pond.

Plants act as "hungry cleaners" in the pond, absorbing nutrients that would otherwise feed algae and keeping the water clear and balanced.

Wetland, Gravel Beds and Bog Filters

Adding gravel beds or bog filters around the pond edges promotes beneficial bacteria growth, helping to break down waste. Picture these as small marshy areas with plants that act as "mini cleaners" absorbing extra nutrients to maintain a healthy pond without chemicals.

When you have the space, constructed wetland filters are one of the best investments you can make. Think of them as sponges for the pond, filtering waste and keeping water clear. I've found that a well-sized wetland filter can last for years before needing a clean-out. With the correct size, you typically need to clean them once after 12 months, and then you can leave them for several years before needing to clean them again. They take advantage of natural processes.

Unlike bog filters or gravel beds, wetland filters are designed for easy cleaning when necessary. Ensure gravel beds and bog filters are sizeable enough to handle waste; otherwise, they can clog over time. Traditional European-style swim ponds use this method for their regeneration zone. Still, these systems are designed for "educated" human immersion (you should refrain from stirring up the bio waste on the base of the pond) with no ornamental pond fish. While some bog filters can be cleaned via small pipes, they must be supervised and cleaned out regularly; you can only leave them for a short time as they will cake up and block, unlike adequately sized constructed wetland filters.

My Time-Saving Tips for Busy Pond Owners

Caring for a pond can seem like a lot of work, but it doesn't have to be! Whether you have a frog pond or a small fish pond, there are clever ways to save time while keeping your pond healthy and beautiful. From my experience in maintaining all my ponds, I've gathered some easy tips to share below. Still, one of the most helpful things I found early on was installing a pitched cover net before the leaves fall. Yes, it looks terrible, but it's less work. I netted many ponds before but found they would sag under the weight of wet leaves (then the leaves would rot and fall in). *Prevention is vital.*

I have included a few tips for more advanced pond owners below.

Automated Pond Care Solutions

Automation cleaning doesn't make a pond filter hands-off, but it does simplify maintenance. You do need to pay attention (more than most think). Automatic cleaning filters are effective when working well but require careful setup and regular attention. Often, you have extensive manuals with lots of small print. These systems suit small, compact spaces but may be best avoided for beginners. Drum filters clean automatically and are loved by experienced koi pool owners. They are, however, still not carefree. Screens still need to be cleaned, and water needs to be automatically topped up.

You need to understand error codes, and the running costs are high compared to constructed wetland filters, but again, they are great for small compact spaces and flush the waste away as soon as the fish defecate. In the season, this can be very quick after eating. Most are kept in a filter house or shed by the pond or pool. I would not recommend these systems for beginners.

Automatic Water Top-Ups

Evaporation is standard in warmer months, but an automatic water topper system keeps the water level stable. The topper adds enough water to keep everything balanced whenever the pond water levels decrease. These devices connect to your home's water source and top up the water as needed. Be careful if you have these systems, as they could hide or mask water loss issues.

Solar-Powered Aerators

Solar aerators are great for smaller ponds, improving oxygenation and reducing algae without needing an external power source. Solar-powered filters are also energy-efficient and ideal for locations with limited access to electricity. Please note the ones you buy off the shelves are only great for small ponds.

Timed Lighting

Timed pond lights or photocell timers enhance your pond's aesthetics and gently remind you of daily or seasonal care needs. I love the convenience of having the lights automatically switch off four hours after dark (with other settings available), allowing me to enjoy the serene glow before settling down for the night. Discover more about this convenient solution at https://waterfeature.shop/lighting-timer.

Low-Impact Pond Design Choices

You can also make a few design choices to help maintenance in the long run. One is choosing eco-friendly setups. Biofilter mats, biodegradable pond treatments and eco-friendly materials promote a balanced ecosystem without harsh chemicals. Think of biofilter mats as a "hotel" for bacteria – bacteria settle on these mats and break down waste, keeping the water clear.

Fewer fish and more plants will also help. Stocking fewer fish means less waste, which reduces maintenance. Instead, aim for a lush variety of plants to filter the water naturally. Another design choice to make is the shades and covers. Plants or structures that shade the pond reduce sunlight exposure, discouraging algae growth. Floating plants like water lilies or a pergola over the pond can also help maintain cooler water temperatures.

Shade and Cover

Plants or structures that shade the pond reduce sunlight exposure, discouraging algae growth. Floating plants like water lilies or a pergola over the pond can also help maintain cooler water temperatures.

Regional Pond Care Tips

Maintenance of a pond can vary greatly depending on your local climate, as factors such as temperature, humidity and seasonal changes significantly affect pond care. Although every pond is unique, I've compiled my top tips to help you prepare for and maintain a thriving pond throughout the year based on what climate you may have.

Temperate Climates

In temperate climates (e.g. the UK), mild winters and warm summers provide a balanced environment for maintaining ponds. In Britain, winters are cool and wet, while summers are warm and wet. My climate rarely experiences extreme heat or cold, drought or strong winds that are common in other regions.

Year-round greenery. Remove tropical plants that can't withstand freezing temperatures before they pollute the water. You can keep some alive in frost-free areas. Choose a mix of evergreen and seasonal pond plants to maintain visual interest and filtration year-round. If there aren't enough plants, algae blooms often occur in spring and early autumn. As the other pond plants are more complex, single-celled algae (green water) might appear.

Winter protection. Temperate ponds may only partially freeze, but preventing complete ice cover is essential.

We don't tend to switch off pond equipment in the UK, so flowing water keeps a hole in the ice in the coldest months. Many fish pool owners moved pumps closer to the filter box outlet to avoid mixing the bottom warmer layers. This also removes the risk of the pools being drained immediately if the plumbing starts leaking at this time of the year. I have also seen small aquarium-size heaters used hanging from polystyrene.

Still-water ponds. You might ask how I keep a hole in the ice on a still-temperate wildlife pond during winter (like the frog pond). A simple floating ice preventer can be ideal. This device is made from polystyrene and is designed in two parts (a top and a bottom). It creates a small air chamber that prevents ice formation in the middle of that spot while allowing essential gas exchange. Float it on the pond's surface, preventing it from freezing solid.

I have also heard about using a tennis or football ball to prevent ice formation, but this information is more from when people had problems with concrete pools cracking in the colder months. The balls move around a little but usually get lodged in a corner or by a pipe, so they just freeze up.

Colder Climates

In colder climates, you'll need to protect your pond.

Switch to winter care. Reduce feeding as temperatures drop, as fish metabolism slows. Most ponds in cold zones need to be winterised, turning off the filtration and bleeding the plumbing dry. These ponds need to be cleaned in the spring to remove all the waste over the winter months. You don't want water in your plumbing to keep it from getting damaged in the freezing weather, causing water to be lost in the spring once you switch everything back on.

Preventing ice formation. Use a cattle trough, stock tank heater, pond heater or de-icer to prevent complete ice cover, with the aid of a bubbler pump or spare pond pump (make sure you have a cage or prefilter on the pump), allowing fish to breathe and gases to escape. If thick ice forms, avoid breaking it manually, as the shock waves can harm fish. I have used a drill or hole saw before. Instead of breaking the ice, you can use a pan or kettle of hot water.

Bringing fish indoors. Consider bringing fish indoors for the winter in shallow ponds or particularly harsh climates. Moving fish to a tank or deeper pond protects them from extreme temperatures. The Japanese koi breeders do this yearly; they have tall, sloped roofs on the fish houses, as they can have 8' 2.4 m of snow. I have seen this with my own eyes.

Hot Climates

Pond care in hot climates centres around managing evaporation and maintaining water quality.

Dealing with sun and dry weather. Positioning your pond in a shaded area helps reduce water loss. Think about where you want to stand in the heat of the day. Do you have any shade in your garden? If not, you can add shade using garden sails or float plants, lowering water temperature and preventing excessive algae growth.

Automated water top-up. Hot climates lead to rapid water loss due to evaporation. An automatic top-up system ensures the water level stays consistent without frequent manual refills. Deeper ponds also tend to be colder, so go deeper to reduce evaporation.

Aeration. Air pumps are essential for maintaining healthy garden ponds in these conditions. Considerable solar panels power up are the best ones I have seen. Solar power charges the batteries, and you can run the compressors from these solar banks via converters. This offers an excellent solution for off-grid locations where the sun can significantly impact oxygen levels. Warm, still pond water holds much less oxygen. Harnessing the sun's energy to circulate the water is the cheapest way to move and cool water.

The Joy of Low-Maintenance Pond Ownership

When I speak with people considering a pond, one of the first questions they often ask is, "How much work will it be?" or, "Do I need a filter? As I don't have power in the garden." Thinking about endless cleaning and battling algae can feel overwhelming; I get it. I thought the same thing when I first started trying to keep fish! I killed far too many in the first few years. I added them to temporary bodies of water, as that was all I thought they needed. I didn't like plants, or anywhere they would hide, but over the years, I've learned that a pond (still or moving) can almost take care of itself with the right design and tools. You can enjoy a few fish without much work. You won't even have to feed them if you do not want to.

As you can see, my ponds are designed to be as hands-off as possible. I now enjoy people's reactions to the enormous fish and watch them start to relax, connecting with nature and not wanting to leave, even on my days off (I invite people over as the ponds and water features are an absolute joy). I only finish the landscaping or gardening on my passion projects, as once the water is in, I sit enjoying life. I often get caught sitting by the ponds in our water feature gardens at POND college (this is our UK-based training centre where we offer classes and workshops on water features). I sit there in the morning, drinking my coffee, listening to the running water – which helps me follow up with emails – and watching the wildlife coming to the ponds. It's so calming. It's all about balance; you need the proper filtration or enough plants to support the aquatic life and a system that works with nature rather than against it.

One of my clients recently upgraded to a more efficient, low-maintenance pond setup, and their experience sums up the benefits beautifully:

"The investment and time spent were well worth it. The skimmer box is a dream – apart from rescuing the odd goldfish! Compared to my old pond, where I was constantly battling blanket weeds and cleaning the pump and filter weekly, I just pulled a few weeds from the waterfall each week. The water clarity is amazing, and my fish couldn't be happier. They even started spawning within weeks!"

With the proper setup, pond maintenance is drastically reduced, letting you enjoy your pond rather than constantly managing it.

A Recap: Road to a Low-Maintenance Pond

Regular maintenance keeps your pond healthy. Cleaning filters regularly, monitoring water quality, and removing debris are simple but effective ways to keep your pond healthy.

Seasonal adjustments make a difference. Adjusting care routines seasonally, from topping up water in summer to preventing ice formation in winter, ensures your pond remains vibrant year-round.

Add the right plants. Incorporating native or local aquatic plants requires less care. They adapt to the climate and thrive naturally in your pond. These plants reduce nutrient buildup and discourage algae, making pond maintenance easier.

Consider automation to save time. Automatic water toppers, solar-powered aerators and other automated solutions can significantly reduce the time spent on upkeep.

Adhere to climate-specific care. Tailoring your pond care to local climate conditions – temperate, cold, or hot – allows you to manage specific challenges efficiently.

- **Temperate Climates (e.g., the UK):** Keep ponds partly ice-free in winter and use evergreen plants for year-round filtration.
- **Colder Climates:** Winterise ponds by turning off filtration, keeping bleeding pipes dry, and using deicers or floating ice preventers to protect fish.
- **Hot Climates:** Shading, deeper ponds, and solar-powered aerators help manage evaporation and oxygen levels in hot climates.

By adopting these simple, low-maintenance strategies, you'll create a beautiful, sustainable pond that takes care of itself for much of the year. Whether you're a busy pond owner or simply looking to minimise upkeep, these tips ensure that pond care remains an enjoyable and stress-free aspect of your gardening routine.

Watch my maintenance and cleaning videos at: https://waterfeature.shop/pond-maintenance-videos for expert guidance. For comprehensive guidance on pond cleaning, consider exploring resources like my beginner's guide to garden pond cleaning: https://anypond.com/garden-pond-cleaning/.

Chapter 8
TROUBLESHOOTING COMMON POND PROBLEMS

Creating a beautiful pond is rewarding, but challenges will inevitably arise. This chapter guides you through tackling pond issues so you can enjoy a beautiful, healthy pond with fewer hassles. As someone who's encountered almost every garden pond problem in the book, I'll guide you through methods for tackling these issues while sharing some lessons I learned the hard way.

My First Pond: Learning Through Trial and Error

In the summer of 1989, at just 11 years old, I decided to build my first pond. With a pocket-money budget funded by six paper rounds, I was determined to learn about fish and create a little oasis in my mum's garden. However, my youthful enthusiasm was tempered by mistakes and lessons that would later guide my pond-building career.

I chose the tightest spot possible, next to a shed and beneath a plum tree – a decision that would lead to many challenges. My budget allowed for a basic PVC liner, a compromise over the more expensive rubber liner I wanted. With that liner, I thought I was ready to start digging, but I hadn't accounted for the garden's slope. To save time and effort, I mounded up the soil on one side, not realising it would destabilise as it settled.

The first problems appeared almost immediately. Garden slabs, which I thought were securely in place, began sliding into the pond as the soil compacted. My attempt to "pack" the soil by jumping on it only worsened things. The deep zone I'd dug for overwintering, positioned without internal support, soon caved in after the first rainfall. The pond was too close to the shed, and debris from the plum tree – including sticky sap and falling leaves – turned the water murky and difficult to maintain.

Despite all these setbacks, that first pond sparked a lifelong passion for garden water features. Each pond I've built since has benefited from the lessons learned during that summer. This experience taught me that a pond is more than just a hole filled with water; it's a carefully planned ecosystem that can bring joy and beauty to a garden for years to come.

So, if you're starting, take the time to plan carefully. Avoid my mistakes, and remember that each challenge can lead to valuable lessons. When I built my first pond, I learned that each choice – from location to materials – has a lasting impact. Thoughtful planning and quality materials set the foundation for a pond that thrives with minimal intervention.

Are ponds a lot of work?

Not at all with the right design. If it's a lot of work, don't blame the pond – blame the pond designer. Flowering aquatic plants in single-pond pots or more extensive patio ponds is, in fact, much easier and more accessible to care for than traditional bedding plants for busy homeowners or professionals. Conventional bedding plants need watering daily, compared to topping up a patio pond once a week (or even monthly).

How to Prevent and Solve Water Quality Issues

Water quality is fundamental for a thriving pond. Cloudy water, algae blooms and oxygen imbalances can quickly disrupt the pond's ecosystem. I remember the frustration of battling algae in one of my early ponds. Watching it overtake the water felt like a losing battle, but I eventually discovered some strategies that made all the difference. Regular monitoring and early intervention are critical. Don't let minor issues become big problems.

Managing Cloudy Water

Cloudy water is usually caused by debris, soil runoff or the settling of a new pond. It can be remedied with water treatments or proper filtration adjustments. Choosing a filter with adequate biological and mechanical capacity is critical. A well-sized filter matched to your pond size can prevent cloudy water and ecosystem imbalances.

Managing Low Oxygen Levels

Insufficient oxygen levels can stress fish and other aquatic life in a pond. To improve oxygenation, consider adding an air pump. If you have a fish pond, install a waterfall or fountain. If it's a wildlife pond, make sure the waterfall or fountain pumps are safe for aquatic life. Oxygen is vital, especially during hot summer days when oxygen levels will drop. It's important to note that the pond's water quality can deteriorate quickly if you only have one filtration pump and no additional oxygen source.

Additionally, using a pond aeration kit can help mitigate predator issues. Pumping air into the water is the cheapest way to move water around a garden pond.

Managing Algae Blooms

Controlling sunlight exposure and nutrient levels can prevent algae growth. I learned that maintaining a balance of pond plants and regularly cleaning the pond is essential to avoiding this persistent problem.

One of the most frustrating challenges I faced in my early years of pond building was managing algae blooms. One summer, I noticed my pond water turning green almost overnight. Algae had taken over, clouding the water and obscuring everything below the surface. I tried every quick fix, from water changes to manually removing algae (by running green water through pillowcases), but nothing made a lasting difference.

After researching and experimenting, I discovered that a combination of factors needed adjustment to keep algae at bay.

Here's what worked:

The right plant balance. I added more submerged and floating plants, like water lilies and oxygenating plants, which helped absorb the excess nutrients that algae feed on. Even in the winter, evergreen pond plants will remove waste. I love watercress also for its colder water growth.

Installing a UV clarifier. I added a UV clarifier to the filtration system for a fish (not needed on ecosystem ponds). The UV light clumps single-celled algae, which are filtered out, helping clear up the water. When I had too many pond fish, a UV was the only way to clear green water. Back in the day, I thought this was magic. In most cases, I have moved away from this chemical filtration as it's not always needed and can mask problems.

Shading the pond. I reduced sunlight exposure by adding an old door over one of my ponds (which didn't look great but certainly worked). Now, I recommend floating plants or islands. If your budget is not a problem, you can get brilliant shade covers or sails. Covering even part of the pond will slow down the algae's growth. If you're on an actual budget, you can float watercress right out of the bag.

Avoiding excess nutrients. I became mindful about feeding the fish as leftover food can contribute to nutrient levels in the water. If fish food is not eaten, it's like boiling vegetables for too long; the nutrients are washed out, and you're better off drinking the vegetable stock. Of course, fish pond owners want to feed their fish, but it's no good if their food is left floating in the pond. Besides overfeeding being the biggest killer of fish, you also inadvertently feed the algae. If you don't remove it, the filter systems might not be able to cope, which then causes water quality issues.

If you have green fingers or live in a rural setting, monitoring nearby fertiliser use closely is important. Fertilisers from lawns or surrounding areas can easily wash into your pond with rainwater, leading to unwanted issues like algae blooms. Be mindful of the soil or fertiliser you use with aquatic plants. Many pond owners successfully grow them in gravel, which can be naturally fertilised by fish waste. To learn more, watch my video at https://waterfeature.shop/pond-plants-gravel.

Once I implemented these strategies, the green water improved dramatically, and a stable, healthy pond emerged. Next was blanket weed in my fish ponds, but that's more about adding treatments (like Bacteria or Multi Clear).

My guidance for algae blooms: Prevention is a process. Achieving clear water requires several small, consistent actions rather than a single fix. Use multiple controls. Combining plant life, shading, UV light, and nutrient management creates a balanced approach to algae control. Natural filtration is key. Plants play a significant role in absorbing nutrients that would otherwise fuel algae growth, helping maintain clear water in the long run.

Dealing with algae taught me that pond maintenance is about working with nature rather than against it. The experience shaped my approach, showing me that algae control becomes much more manageable when all elements are balanced.

Managing Common Issues of the Pond Pump

Consider the pond pump, which is the beating heart of your pond ecosystem. It circulates water, distributing oxygen and nutrients to plants and fish while driving waste towards the filtration system. Just as our hearts circulate blood to keep us alive, the pump keeps the pond's blood "well water" moving, preventing stagnation and supporting a healthy, balanced environment.

Choosing the Right Pond Pump

Selecting the right pump size and type is critical to avoiding stagnant areas or excessive water movement that can disrupt the ecosystem.

Types of Pond Pumps

Each type of pump has a specific role, so selecting the right one ensures efficient operation and minimises maintenance.

Pump Type	Best For	Key Features	Ideal Use Case
Feature Pumps	Decorative water features and fountains	Propels water upwards for visual interest	Adding beauty with fountains or spouts
Filter Pumps	Fish ponds	Direct water to a biological filter to process solid waste	Maintaining clean, healthy fish ponds
Eco Pumps	Smaller ponds	Energy-efficient, designed for low-level but high water circulation	Reducing running costs in small ponds
Solid Handling Pumps	Ponds with high leaf fall or organic debris	Heavy-duty pumps that manage larger debris without clogging	Managing ponds with heavy organic material
Pond Powerheads	Fish ponds requiring targeted water movement	Low-voltage internal pumps create directional water flow, enriching the environment for aquatic life.	Enhancing fish health and pond oxygenation

My guidance for pond pumps: Choose a pump suited to your pond's size and design. Avoid undersized pumps that can cause stagnation, and use high-quality pumps with solid warranties for reliable performance. For larger ponds, consider using two pumps as a backup system.

Managing Common Issues of Pond Filtration

A healthy pond relies on a well-functioning filtration system, which acts as the pond's digestive and cleansing organs. Mechanical filters operate like a stomach, capturing large debris, while biological filters resemble the liver and kidneys, breaking down dissolved waste to keep the water balanced.

Mechanical Filter = The Stomach

The skimmer, or mechanical filter, acts like a stomach, capturing and holding debris such as leaves and fish waste before it can clog other parts of the system. Regular cleaning keeps it effective, as a clogged filter leads to poor water clarity and places extra strain on the filtration system.

The mechanical filter does two things: It captures debris, preventing leaves and large particles from reaching other filtration components, and it holds waste for further processing, allowing the biological filter to process more negligible dissolved waste.

Biological Filter = The Liver and Kidneys

The biological filter, often found in a waterfall filter, contains beneficial bacteria to help detoxify the pond. These bacteria break down harmful substances such as ammonia and nitrites, creating a safe environment for fish and plants.

Bacteria in biological filters process toxins, converting toxic substances into harmless compounds. This process helps balance and maintain the water by removing dissolved waste, enhancing conditions for aquatic life.

Filter Maintenance and Waste Management

Proper maintenance of mechanical and biological filters ensures balanced water quality and helps prevent nutrient overload, contributing to algae blooms and poor water quality.

- **Mechanical Filters**: These filters capture solids before the water reaches the biological stage and need regular cleaning to remain effective.
- **Biological Filters**: To preserve beneficial bacteria, maintain a hands-off approach. Clean only when necessary, about once every four to six weeks, or less frequently if the waste load is low.

My guidance for pond filtration: Balance maintenance for both filter types to ensure a thriving ecosystem. Mechanical filters should be cleared regularly, and biological filters should not be disturbed too often.

Preventing Nutrient Overload in Your Pond

Excess nutrients from overfeeding fish or accumulating organic debris stress the pond's ecosystem and encourage algae growth. Efficient filtration and mindful feeding help manage waste effectively.

My guidance for maintaining pond nutrients: Follow feeding guidelines and regularly clear the pond of leaves and debris. This prevents the nutrients from building up.

Plumbing Considerations for Pond Efficiency

Leaks or plumbing blockages – seen as the pond's arteries – can hinder the pond's efficiency. Opt for flexible PVC pipes to reduce head pressure and promote smooth water flow. Avoid sharp bends or reduced pipe sizes, which can obstruct circulation.

My guidance for plumbing: Keep plumbing wide and smooth to avoid blockages. Flexible pipes with fewer joints reduce friction and maintain steady water flow, like a racetrack with gentle curves rather than sharp 90-degree bends forcing the water to back up (like racing cars).

Personal Reflections and Key Lessons

Some of my earliest experiences with pond troubleshooting have stayed with me, reinforcing the value of quick action and persistence.

The Tale of the Oversized Pond and the Undersized Filter

I was thrilled to set everything up in one of my early pond projects, but I made a critical misstep: I underestimated the filter's capacity for the pond's size. The pump I chose was too powerful for the undersized filter, creating a constant flow of water that rushed through without allowing the filter to trap waste properly. Despite my adjustments, the water remained murky, and the pond struggled to stay balanced.

After several attempts to fix the problem, I realised I needed a filter that matched the pond's volume. I replaced it with a larger filter designed for the pond's water capacity, and almost immediately, the water began to clear up. The ecosystem stabilised, and I could see the difference that the correct filtration made.

My Guidance for Right-Sizing the Equipment:

Balance is essential. Ensuring your filter and pump are correctly sized for your pond's volume is crucial to maintaining clear, healthy water.

Avoid overloading. Excessive water flow can negatively impact a filter's efficiency, creating murky water and an unhealthy pond ecosystem. When water moves too quickly through a filter, it lacks sufficient time to capture debris effectively, resulting in inadequate cleaning. This rapid movement, like water rushing through multiple chimneys, prevents proper filtration and compromises pond water quality.

Plan ahead. Choosing the right equipment first will save you headaches, resources, and frustration. Get a pond kit or ask for help.

This experience was a turning point in my understanding of pond mechanics. Getting the equipment right is essential for clear water and a balanced and thriving pond environment. So, if you're dealing with murky water, remember that size matters!

Bringing My Fish Back from the "Dead"

One afternoon, when I was young, I checked on the fish in my first pond. I was excited as I had just bought some golden orfe the day before. When I went to feed them, only five of the six new ones came up. I pushed into my fish tunnels (plastic waste pipes, really, but they worked!) but no, they were all empty. I finally spotted my missing orfe lying on the grass about five meters from the pond, completely still and looking entirely lifeless.

My heart sank, but then I saw the faintest flicker of movement in its eye and a slight opening of its mouth. I felt a surge of hope and yelled, "It's alive!"

I ran down to the house. Under the carport, I filled a bucket with tap water and grabbed an aquarium air pump to oxygenate the water out of the shed. I carefully placed my orfe in the bucket, its body stiff and floating on its side. One of my mum's friends, who happened to be visiting, said, "It's gone, Mark, come on mate, it's a waste of time." My mum gently tried to reassure me that there was nothing more I could do. But I wasn't giving up. She told her friend to let me play. Setting up a bucket was the least I could do. At this point, I wished I had another pond. I kept thinking, "What's the best thing to do?" We were due to go for a walk around the country park. I didn't want to put the dying fish back into my pond, as I knew a dead fish would pollute the water, and others would die.

For 20 minutes, nothing changed. But then, almost magically, my orfe started to stir just before we were meant to get into the car for the park. Its body had righted itself and began to move its gills normally. Everyone was shocked, and so was I. It was like magic! My golden orfe had returned to life. I wasn't wasting my time. I felt very smug and happy I had acted quickly. After the walk, I moved the fish back to the garden pond and thought about a new pond setup for sick fish – well, a hospital tank.

My Guidance If Fish Jump Out:

Persistence and patience. Even when the situation looks bleak, patience and quick thinking can make all the difference.

Pond fish are surprisingly resilient. Although they can be fragile, they can sometimes recover if given a supportive environment.

Environment matters. The quick action of getting oxygenated water was crucial, showing how sensitive fish are to their surroundings and the care they receive.

That day, I learned the value of persistence and never giving up, even when others might say it's a lost cause. It also reminded me of how sensitive fish are to their environment – a lesson that has stayed with me through every pond I've built and every fish I've cared for.

Quick action, persistence and patience can sometimes lead to surprising outcomes, even in pond care.

The Pond Leak Mystery: Harder Than Finding a "Needle in a Haystack"

Diagnosing pond water loss is like searching for a needle in a haystack – with a twist. Imagine looking for a needle, but you don't know how many, whether one or twenty, the size, whether it's a tiny pin or a massive knitting needle, or someone is telling you there is a needle, but you're not entirely sure the needle even exists in the first place. Often, water loss isn't caused by a puncture but by a combination of hidden issues like leaks in filtration, plumbing, low edges on streams or small cracks in concrete ponds.

One day, I was called to consult on a pond. The pond owner was sure I'd accidentally punctured his pond liner using a garden cane to measure the pond's depth (during a free consultation). The water level had dropped since my visit, and he was convinced my simple depth check caused the problem. I suggested we troubleshoot systematically. First, I advised him to turn off all the equipment, refill the pond to the top, and monitor the water level overnight without any pumps or filters running. This would rule out whether the issue was with the liner or something in the setup. The next day, he called back, frustrated that the water level had dropped even more.

Determined to find the cause of the issue, I returned to scrutinise everything. As I checked each component, I noticed something unusual about his filter. The rubber seal was missing – a small but essential piece that creates a watertight connection and prevents leaks. When I mentioned it, he admitted he'd recently cleaned the filter after my visit and may have accidentally removed the seal. We searched everywhere for it, but it was nowhere to be found.

Luckily, I had a spare seal with me. I installed it and asked him to monitor the water level for 24 hours. Sure enough, the pond held water perfectly. The culprit had been a tiny missing seal, not a puncture.

My Guidance When Faced With a Mystery:

Don't jump to conclusions. Before assuming the worst, take the time to inspect every part of the setup. Sometimes, the problem isn't as evident as it appears.

Follow a systematic approach. Break down the problem by testing each component individually – like turning off equipment to see if the issue is with the liner itself.

Looking for the hidden "needles." Leaks are often caused by minor issues, such as a missing seal or a loose fitting, rather than a significant liner problem.

Check out my YouTube videos to learn more about locating and fixing leaks. These tutorials will enhance your skills and provide practical solutions. If you're experiencing water loss, watch my video, where I set up five different tests to help my team identify the problem. Although the video focuses on 'How to Find a Problem with a Waterfall,' the same principles apply to ponds and waterfall basins. The first step is always the 24-hour test. Watch it now at https://waterfeature.shop/pond-leak-videos.

Fixing Our Family Doctor's Pond Pump at 13

When I was 13, I got to help with a pond problem at our family doctor's home. My dad and the doctor were close friends and often went on long road runs together. While my dad was chatting about getting ready for a run, the doctor mentioned that his pond pump was giving him trouble. Knowing my interest in ponds, my dad offered to bring me over to take a look.

When we arrived, I inspected the pump and quickly saw the issue: It was designed for a fountain and did not have a filtration system. It was also completely clogged with debris. Water struggled to pass through, and the pump had overheated to the point that the casing was visibly warped. Inside, the impeller was barely turning, unable to circulate water as it should.

I carefully cleaned the pump, removed all the accumulated muck, and thoroughly checked the impeller. After reassembling everything, I switched it on, and the pump whirred to life – with a much stronger flow than ever. The doctor was very impressed. He was amazed that such a young lad could get his pump working again and better than before! After replacing it with the proper filter pump, he even gave me the fountain pump, although it was way too big for any of my ponds back then.

My Guidance if Your Pump Keeps Stopping:

Match the pump to its purpose. Not all pumps are created equal. Fountain pumps are designed for aesthetics, while solid-handling pond pumps handle filtration and need a sturdier setup to hold debris.

Regular maintenance is essential. Clogged pumps lead to overheating and potential failure, so cleaning them regularly can prevent more significant issues.

Attention to small details matters. From choosing the correct type of pump to regular upkeep, small details can significantly affect your pond's performance.

If you're ever in doubt, regular maintenance can often save the day!

The Key Lessons

I want you to take away the most critical points from this chapter: planning, problem-solving and ecosystem balance.

Planning: Thoughtful Design and Preparation

Good planning is like laying a strong foundation for your pond. It paves the way for a beautiful, low-maintenance water feature you can enjoy without worry.

Location matters. Position your pond away from trees. This simple step can drastically reduce debris and keep your maintenance routine light.

Quality over quantity. Invest in top-notch materials. Durable liners, reliable pumps and efficient filters might cost more upfront but will save you time and trouble in the long run.

Right size, right fit. Ensure your pumps and filters appropriately match the size of your pond. This will ensure everything runs smoothly and efficiently.

Problem-Solving: A Systematic Approach

When challenges arise, take a deep breath – solving them is just a step-by-step process away. Here's how you can tackle issues effectively:

Start with the basics. Methodically check each component of your pond setup, from plumbing to seals. Don't jump to conclusions before investigating thoroughly.

Simple fixes first. Sometimes, the solution is easier than you think! Clean your filter or check for low edges where water leaks; these minor adjustments can make a big difference.

Dig deeper. Investigate underlying issues like nutrient buildup or mismatched equipment. Often, these hidden problems are the culprits behind your pond woes.

Ecosystem Balance: Long-Term Success

A harmonious ecosystem pond stays cleaner, brings clarity, supports aquatic life and requires less effort. Here's how to achieve that balance:

Plant power. Integrate aquatic plants into your pond. They help absorb excess nutrients and provide shade, reducing the odds of stubborn algae growth.

Feeding wisely. Monitor your fish's feeding habits. Overfeeding can lead to waste and nutrient overload, so stick to a balanced feeding routine.

Multiple defences for water clarity. Using a mix of algae control methods for crystal-clear water. UV clarifiers (if it's a pool, not a pond), adequate aeration and proper filtration create a robust defence against algae buildup.

Chapter 9
THE POND AS A FAMILY PROJECT

Designing a family-friendly pond creates an engaging and educational space that is enjoyable and safe for children and pets. By thoughtfully incorporating safety features and interactive elements, you can make a tranquil yet secure haven for your family. This chapter is especially relevant to families seeking to balance beauty with practicality, providing tips and ideas for creating a pond that is as safe as it is inviting.

Ponds offer opportunities for children and adults to connect with nature in their gardens. From observing dragonflies to splashing in a shallow zone, these moments foster creativity, curiosity and quality family time. However, safety is a natural concern for parents and pet owners. This chapter will guide you in designing a pond that not only minimises risks but also maximises enjoyment.

Practical Tips for a Safe and Enjoyable Pond

Include a splash pad or play area. Interactive water zones, like splash pads or shallow streams, allow children to engage with water safely. Floating toys, filling buckets or simply enjoying the sight and sound of moving water creates a magical and low-risk experience. Adding sensory elements, such as fragrant plants like mint or lavender near the edges, enriches the experience for children.

Shallow zones for play. Shallow areas encourage safe exploration and play while reducing the risk of deeper water. Make sure that you have gradual depth transitions. It helps to design the pond's edges with gently sloping shallow areas, making it safe for kids to dip their hands or toes. You can also include wading areas by laying smooth pebbles or flat stones in shallow zones, creating inviting areas for kids to interact with water.

Easy-exit areas. Incorporate stepping stones or wooden steps as visual features and safety measures. These allow children and pets to exit the water quickly if they accidentally enter.

No standing water in water features. Pondless water features – streams, waterfalls, or fountains – offer all the charm of water without standing pools. These features minimise risks while adding a dynamic, naturalistic element to your garden.

Natural barriers and borders. Soft barriers, such as dense plants or low fences, create attractive yet practical boundaries around the pond. A garden edge filled with rocks or low-growing shrubs can act as a buffer zone, slowing children and pets from approaching too quickly.

Strong covers only. If you choose to use a cover, ensure it can support the weight of an adult. Secure plastic grids under the water surface allow circulation while preventing access to deeper areas.

Education and Supervision

Even with safety measures in place, education and supervision remain essential. Be sure to teach water safety. Establish clear rules about when and how children can interact with the pond. Ensure that young children and pets can only access the pond with adult supervision, ensuring their safety and enjoyment.

Take the Time to Understand and Mitigate Risks

Assess potential risks. Consider who will use the space – children, pets or visitors – and how they might interact with your garden.

Assess hazards. Look for steep edges, slippery surfaces or deep pond sections.

Check local regulations. Visit your council's website or contact the planning department to ensure depth and fencing rules compliance. Consulting insurance providers or pond professionals can also provide helpful advice. Local laws may require fencing or barriers for ponds exceeding specific depths.

Enhance safety and beauty. Dense planting or decorative fencing can improve safety and enhance the aesthetics of your garden.

By identifying risks early, you can create solutions that enhance your pond's safety and beauty, ensuring you and your loved ones peace of mind.

By incorporating these thoughtful design elements, your family-friendly pond becomes more than just a garden feature – it becomes a space where creativity, connection and relaxation thrive. Encourage your children to name the fish, observe nature or learn about aquatic plants and ecosystems. These experiences create lasting memories and deepen their appreciation for the natural world.

With careful planning, your pond will be a safe, enchanting retreat that grows alongside your family.

A Rewarding Collaboration with the Knowles Family

One of the most fulfilling wildlife pond projects I've ever worked on was with the Knowles family. The Knowles couple, both doctors, wanted a safe, interactive and educational pond for their children while preserving the natural beauty they cherished from their childhoods. They envisioned a space where their kids could splash, explore and learn about nature while pitching in with simple pond tasks like netting leaves.

When they moved into their home, the garden featured a small, shallow pond that teemed with frogs in spring but quickly filled with leaves and waste. Surrounded by concrete and paving slabs, this pond had become more of a source of frustration than joy. Tadpoles appeared each year, only to vanish before they could turn into froglets. Clearly, the pond needed a redesign to become the family-friendly, environmentally conscious space they dreamed of.

Designing with Family in Mind

Our first step was reimagining the pond as part of a larger, playful ecosystem. We introduced a standalone splash pad, which became a cornerstone of the project. The splash pad was a shallow, smooth-stoned sink with two bubbling water features: one fed through a millstone and another via a simple jet. The water play area encouraged the children to fill buckets, water the vegetable garden and cool off during summer.

This feature wasn't just fun – it was educational. It introduced the children to the movement of water and its role in gardening and conservation. The millstone fountain could connect bamboo raceways, turning the feature into an interactive experiment.

From the splash pad, a shallow stream meandered through the garden. Though it appeared connected to the main pond, the stream was separate for safety. It featured small cobble-made "dams," perfect for floating leaf boats or creating raceways. Kept at a depth of just 15 cm, it provided a safe and exciting way for the children to explore water flow and currents while having fun.

We installed an underground rainwater harvesting system beneath the splash pad and stream to make the design even more eco-friendly. This system collected rainwater from one side of the house, filtered it and stored it in the splash pad, stream and garden. The overflow was directed into the main pond, ensuring the family's water play was sustainable and resource-efficient.

The main pond was designed with shallow zones along the edges, featuring smooth stones and pebbles for safe wading. These areas were deep enough to support tadpoles and froglets, helping to bring wildlife back into the garden. Around the perimeter, lush plants and low rocks created a natural barrier, slowing the children's approach while keeping leaves at bay.

The Knowles appreciated how this combination of beauty and practicality made the wildlife pond feel like a seamless part of their garden. The children loved naming the tadpoles and eagerly awaited each spring's new visitors.

A Pond That Grows with the Family

The pond quickly became a cherished family space. It allowed the children to connect with nature and sparked countless lessons in water conservation, wildlife and teamwork. Their parents delighted in seeing them play, learn, and even take on responsibilities like watering the garden and clearing leaves from the pond.

The first weekend after the project's completion, the kids couldn't resist building an elaborate raceway – draining all the water out of the splash basin in the process! This was a humorous and valuable lesson in water management. Over the next 18 months, the family sent me countless photos and videos documenting the wildlife they discovered and the memories they created together.

The Knowles' pond was more than just a water feature – it became a hub for exploration, creativity and connection. The design will continue to evolve as their children grow, from playful splash pad days to serene evenings by the pond.

This project encapsulates what makes water gardening so rewarding: creating spaces that bring families closer to nature and each other, blending beauty with practicality and fun. For the Knowles, their pond isn't just a feature in the garden; it's the heart of their family's outdoor life.

Getting Kids Involved in Pond Care

A garden pond is not just a beautiful water feature – it's an interactive, educational tool that sparks curiosity, teaches valuable life skills and fosters a sense of responsibility in children. Involving kids in pond care transforms your garden into a living classroom and an opportunity for meaningful family bonding.

The Educational Values of a Garden Pond

A pond provides hands-on learning experiences beyond the classroom, offering insights into biology, ecology and even physics. Observing the pond allows children to explore nature at their own pace while developing an appreciation for the natural world.

Aquatic Wildlife Discovery

Teach kids how to spot and understand the roles of various pond creatures within the ecosystem. For example:

- **Frogs**: Look for clumps of spawn and watch tadpoles transform. Introduce them to the fascinating fact that tadpoles eat algae before transitioning to meatier diets (feed processed chicken slices).

- **Newts**: Spring evenings with a torch reveal their courting dance. Kids can learn to spot single eggs tucked in aquatic plants. If lucky, they can watch the newts dance in the spring.
- **Toads**: Point out their grumpy appearance and how they crawl rather than hop like frogs.
- **Dragonflies**: Teach kids to look for exuviae – the shed skins of dragonflies – and watch them hunt on the wing.
- **Fish**: Show how ornamental fish can dominate an ecosystem, eating everything from snails to tadpoles. Highlight why wildlife ponds and ornamental fish don't mix.

Encourage kids to keep a wildlife journal, tracking the creatures they see over time and how the pond changes with the seasons.

How Ponds Teach Children About Wildlife and Ecosystems

A pond is a gateway to understanding the delicate balance needed to sustain life. By engaging in pond care, children develop an appreciation for biodiversity and learn how their actions impact the environment.

- **Encouraging biodiversity**. Show how adding oxygenating plants or water lilies provides shelter and food for pond creatures.

- **Understanding habitats.** Help them observe how animals, plants and water interact to create a thriving ecosystem.
- **Respect for nature.** Watching their efforts lead to healthy plants and wildlife fosters respect and a sense of stewardship for the natural world.
- **Cause and effect.** Teach kids how overfeeding fish or neglecting debris removal can upset the pond's balance, affecting water quality and inhabitants.

Engaging with nature also builds patience and discipline. The rewards of observing thriving wildlife teach children the value of care and consistency.

Fun Activities to Engage Children

Make pond care exciting and educational with these creative ideas:

- **Treasure Hunts**: Create a list of common pond plants, leaf shapes, insects and animals to spot around the pond. Add painted stones or "hidden treasures" for younger children to find.
- **Mini Habitats**: Let kids build frog shelters or place branches and flat rocks for dragonflies to perch on. Teach them to observe without disturbing the wildlife.
- **Nature Journals**: Encourage kids to record their observations and discoveries, fostering a deeper connection to the ecosystem.

- **Pond Monitoring**: To give them a sense of ownership, involve them in checking water clarity, counting fish, or observing plant growth.

Projects for Young Teens

Maintaining a pond offers valuable lessons in balance, consistency, and attention to detail.

Assign age-appropriate tasks such as:

- **Pocket Money Jobs**: Skimming leaves, cleaning filters and checking water levels.
- **Feeding Fish**: Teenagers often enjoy this task and do it for free, but it can teach responsibility. The fish must get food when needed, and if they truly own the task, they will have to ask others to cover for them when they are away on holiday.
- **Troubleshooting**: Teach them to think critically by identifying and solving pond issues like algae growth or equipment malfunctions.

Responsibility and Ownership

Involving children in pond care helps them develop accountability. Whether feeding the fish or skimming leaves, every task fosters a sense of responsibility. They learn that their actions directly impact the health and beauty of the pond.

By nurturing their curiosity and involving them in pond care, you're giving your children more than a hobby – you're instilling a lifelong respect for nature and a deeper understanding of the world around them.

These lessons, learned through hands-on experience, will stay with them as they grow, turning your pond into a family treasure and a source of inspiration for years.

Now that we've explored creating a safe and enjoyable pond environment for families, we'll move on to practical advice on keeping your pond thriving. Hence, you will continue to enjoy your pond for years to come.

Chapter 10
EMBRACING THE POND LIFESTYLE

Owning a pond is about more than just adding water to your garden – it's about creating a lifestyle that fosters connection, creativity and calm. Imagine sitting by the water at sunrise, hearing the gentle splash of a fountain while dragonflies skim the surface. Whether large or small, every pond can transform your garden into a sanctuary.

Reflecting on my journey since 1989, ponds have brought me immense fulfilment – building and maintaining them and seeing the joy they bring to others. A client once shared how her pond became her refuge during a difficult time, where she could reset and find peace. Another client told me about her granddaughter, who spent hours sitting by their pond, naming the fish and marvelling at their world. These stories are constant reminders that a pond is more than just a feature; it's a living, breathing gift.

I want to take a moment to remember a late friend, Scott Hammond, who passed away in May 2017 from cancer. Scott, from Ellensburg, Washington, inspired me to write this chapter about embracing the pond lifestyle. He would often say, "God is a funny guy." Scott owned a company called Aquascape by Blue Creek and recorded a video about what we aquatic artists truly create. It's not just a water feature; it's a lifestyle – a *good* lifestyle.

One story Scott told has stayed with me ever since. A couple had recently completed their pond, and Scott visited to check on the project. He found two chairs moved from the patio onto the lawn, positioned for the perfect view of the water feature. Between them sat a table with a bowl of grapes, some crackers and cheese, and two glasses of wine held in goblet stakes planted firmly in the ground. Scott said, "I realised that what we had given them wasn't just a pond – it was time together. Quality time in a serene, tranquil environment where they could reconnect."

Scott also shared a touching moment with another client who was initially concerned about her seven-year-old granddaughter being around the pond. To her surprise, the little girl spent four hours sitting on what Scott affectionately called the "butt rock" at the edge of the pond. She named all the fish, created stories about their personalities, and insisted that her lunch be brought so she wouldn't have to leave her particular spot. That rock became a place of discovery, peace and joy for a child.

These stories illustrate a pond's profound impact on life – creating moments that nurture relationships, foster creativity and provide solace. Every pond has the potential to become a gift far greater than water and stone. We should cherish these silver and gold moments, for they genuinely define the magic of pond ownership.

Defining "Pond Perfection"

For beginners, "pond perfection" can feel intimidating, but it's essential to understand that perfection is deeply personal. It isn't about having the most extensive or expensive pond. Instead, it's about creating a space that feels right for you – a simple wildlife sanctuary buzzing with activity, a serene corner for quiet meditation or a vibrant garden centrepiece that sparks conversation with your friends and family.

Start Small, Dream Big

Many beginners worry that their first pond won't measure up to their vision, but perfection doesn't happen overnight. Start with small, achievable goals that align with your interests and lifestyle. Focus on what brings you joy.

Observe the wildlife. Attract dragonflies, frogs or birds to your pond by incorporating shallow edges, floating plants or marginal vegetation. Watching these creatures thrive is a joyful reminder of the connection between water and life.

Enjoy the moment. Spend time sitting by your pond, listening to the gentle sound of water or reflecting on the space you've created. This peaceful time can become a cherished part of your daily routine.

Experiment gradually. Try introducing different aquatic plants or new fish. Watching a lily bloom or a koi glide through the water is exciting and rewarding. I still love the sound a koi makes when feeding, and it never gets boring. These days, it's more rewarding to explain the different personalities of my pet fish to people visiting my garden.

The key is to embrace the process. While starting small is essential, dreaming big gives you a vision to grow into. Let your imagination explore the possibilities, even as you take small, steady steps. Every pond begins with a ripple, and those ripples gradually build toward something extraordinary.

Evolving Over Time

Your first pond doesn't need to be your last. Many pond owners discover their vision grows as their confidence and understanding deepen. I've seen countless clients transform their initial "good" pond into something "better" or even "best" over time.

One family began with a simple wildlife pond, hoping to attract frogs and insects. They added a stream to enhance movement and sound a few years later. Eventually, their "final" pond (for now) became a stunning multi-level ecosystem with koi and underwater lighting. Each stage brought new joy and fulfilment, and the pond evolved alongside them.

As you explore these small steps, you'll find new possibilities, guiding you toward what your pond could become.

Let Go of Perfectionism

It's natural to want everything to be "just right," but the truth is that every pond has imperfections – and that's okay. Think of your pond as a living project rather than a fixed achievement.

A liner that shows around the edges, a plant that grows too wild or a small patch of algae are all part of the learning process. Each challenge teaches you something new about your pond and yourself. Embrace the imperfections – they testify to your growth as a pond owner.

One of my clients affectionately called her first pond her "ugly baby." While she knew it wasn't flawless, it was hers, and she loved it deeply. Over time, she made minor improvements, and that "ugly baby" grew into a feature she was immensely proud of.

Celebrate Every Stage

Whether your pond is a modest beginning or an elaborate dream feature, it deserves celebration. Every step of the journey – from digging the first hole to seeing your first water lily bloom – is a milestone worth recognising. Think of each stage as part of a larger story that reflects your creativity, care and connection to nature.

Your pond will never be "done," and that's its beauty. Instead of chasing perfection, focus on progress. Appreciate what you've built and look forward to what's next. Each challenge, whether algae growth or a plant spreading too wildly, provides an opportunity to learn more about your pond and refine your approach. These lessons make your pond journey uniquely yours.

Every pond build tells a unique story; the most meaningful chapter in that story is the one you're writing now. Just as I've reflected on my journey – returning to where my passion for ponds began – I encourage you to celebrate your progress and dream about your next chapter.

My Sense of Fulfilment

Over the years, I've had the privilege of designing and building ponds for friends, families, schools and small communities. Each has a unique story that reminds me why I love what I do. From a simple patio pond offering solace to a busy family to helping others design seven-figure water features transforming sprawling estates and extensive private gardens, the true magic of these projects lies not in their size or complexity but in the connections they foster.

Each pond I've built or designed has become more than just a water feature; it's been a sanctuary for reflection, a hub for family bonding or even a tool for learning and exploration. Knowing that my work can create spaces where people reconnect with nature and each other fills me with immense pride.

A Personal Transformation

One of the most transformative moments in my career came during the 2016 Hampton Court Flower Show. After winning the runner-up Best in Show, I was surrounded by gardening press and visitors eager to ask questions. Amid this buzz, a young boy approached me wide-eyed and said, "If I were an ant, I would want to live there."

His words stopped me in my tracks. At that moment, he wasn't just admiring the design of the water features but imagining a world within it, and he wanted to take the time to explain how my garden had made him feel or how my level of detail had inspired him. This child saw something magical, a place where creativity and nature could harmonise to spark the imagination. A world of pure imagination

At that moment, I felt like the "Willy Wonka of Water Features," crafting enchanting spaces that inspire wonder and connection. It reminded me why I do what I do –

not just to build ponds and water features but to create invitations for others to dream, explore and connect; living there, you'll be free if you truly wish to be.

Such moments – whether a child's imagination is sparked by a water garden, a family gathering around their pond, silver and gold moments or a school project exploring aquatic life – remind me that ponds are about more than water and stone. They're about building bridges between people, pets, nature and the power of endless imagination.

This sense of fulfilment drives me to keep going, helping more people create spaces that resonate with more people and leave a lasting impact. Each pond, no matter the size, carries the potential to transform not just a garden but the lives of those who enjoy it.

Celebrating Your Achievement

Building a pond is no small feat. It requires creativity, effort and care, but the rewards far outweigh the challenges. Whether you've constructed a small wildlife pond teeming with frogs and dragonflies or a grand koi pond with flowing waterfalls, take a moment to celebrate your accomplishment.

Your pond isn't just a garden feature – it's a testament to your vision, persistence and love for nature. It's a space that reflects who you are and the connections you wish to nurture, whether with family, friends, or the natural world.

The Joys of Ponds

Ponds bring countless rewards that go beyond their physical beauty. They enhance your life in ways that might surprise you.

Connection. Your pond creates a serene space to bond with loved ones. Whether feeding the fish with your children or enjoying a quiet evening by the water with your partner, these moments become cherished memories.

Inspiration. Ponds are havens for creativity. Watching fish dart through the water or seeing a dragonfly hovering over a lily pad can spark ideas, dreams and a deeper appreciation for the world around you.

Fulfilment. A pond isn't static; it's a living, evolving project. As you care for it, make adjustments, and watch it grow, it reflects your journey – a source of pride and joy that develops alongside you.

Celebrate Every Milestone

The pond lifestyle is about appreciating the little moments as much as the big ones. Watching your first lily bloom is an unforgettable experience and a sign that your pond is thriving. Seeing your fish flourish is a testament to your care and attention and a tangible reminder of your success. Most encompassing are the quiet and peaceful moments you spend by the water, listening to its gentle ripples as you are embraced by immense calm and satisfaction.

Each of these milestones deserves to be celebrated, no matter how small they may seem. Your pond is an extension of you – a place that grows, changes and flourishes just as you do.

So, take pride in what you've built. Every ripple, every bloom and every splash is part of your story. Celebrate it. Let it inspire you to dream bigger, explore more and enjoy the countless joys your pond will continue to bring.

Ways to Continue Your Pond Journey

Your pond journey doesn't end with your first project – it's only the beginning. As your confidence and curiosity grow, you'll likely start dreaming about ways to expand, enhance and refine your water feature. The beauty of pond ownership lies in its endless possibilities. Each new addition or improvement brings fresh challenges, rewards and opportunities to connect with nature.

Ideas for Growth

Here are a few ways to take your pond to the next level.

Expand. If you've outgrown your first pond, consider increasing its size. A larger pond allows for more fish, plants, and features, creating a richer ecosystem and a more dynamic focal point for your garden.

Experiment. Try introducing new elements to your pond, such as lighting to enjoy its beauty at night, a cascading waterfall for sound and movement, or exotic aquatic plants to diversify your features.

Innovate. Explore modern tools like smart pond devices that help with water quality or eco-friendly upgrades like adding a small solar-powered pump with a fountain. These advancements make maintenance more accessible while keeping your pond sustainable.

Learn and Grow

Every addition is a chance to learn something new. Whether you're testing a new plant, installing a stream or tweaking your pond's ecosystem, these small experiments help deepen your understanding and appreciation of water gardening.

For example, one client started with a small koi pond but wanted to enhance its aesthetics. They added a bubbling stream that meandered through their garden, creating a soothing soundscape. A few years later, they installed underwater lighting, turning their pond into a stunning evening retreat. Each step brought them closer to their vision of perfection and gave them new ways to engage with their pond.

Keep the Journey Fresh

The pond lifestyle is dynamic – it evolves as you do. As your skills grow, so will your imagination and willingness to try new things. The key is approaching each stage with curiosity and a sense of adventure.

Start small. Adding a new plant or feature doesn't need to be a grand project. Small changes can make a big difference and inspire further exploration.

Adapt to your needs. Your pond can change as your life does. A wildlife pond for your children may evolve into a serene retreat for relaxation or a vibrant space for entertaining friends.

Celebrate progress. No matter how small, every enhancement adds to your pond's story. Enjoy the process as much as the results.

Your pond journey is unique to you. Each step forward builds on the last, creating a richer, more rewarding experience. As you grow your pond, remember that it's not just about the destination – it's about enjoying every moment along the way.

The Pond Community

Water gardening becomes truly fulfilling when shared with others. Joining a pond community offers endless inspiration, support and meaningful connections. Whether you're a novice seeking guidance or a seasoned enthusiast eager to share your expertise, joining a community amplifies the joy of your pond journey.

Join the https://waterfeature.shop/community to connect with pond lovers of all levels. Our community is a space to share, learn and celebrate water gardening. Here, you'll find encouragement, expert advice and inspiring stories about the beauty and joy of ponds.

Your Invitation

Take your pond journey to the next level by joining this vibrant community. Here's how you can participate:

Share your milestones. Post photos, stories or videos of your pond's progress. Whether it's a blooming water lily or a creative feature you've added, your journey can inspire others.

Ask questions. Seek advice from fellow pond owners and experts who understand the joys and challenges of water gardening.

Find encouragement. Celebrate your successes and receive support through challenges.

By joining the community, you'll discover a network of people who share your passion and can help you grow as a pond enthusiast.

One of My Favourite Connections

Over the years, I've witnessed how ponds bring people together unexpectedly. Clients often tell me they feel like

I've become part of their family – a trusted advisor who shares their excitement and accomplishments.

One client even called me "Heston Blumenthal, but with water features" because of the creativity and detail I pour into every project. Moments like these remind me how deeply ponds connect us. Your pond can have the same effect, transforming your garden, relationships and community.

The pond lifestyle creates profound connections, from clients who feel like family to strangers who become friends over their love of water gardening.

Reflect and Celebrate

Take a moment to reflect on your pond journey so far:

What have you learned or overcome?

How has your pond enriched your life?

What moments stand out as the most memorable?

Celebrate each step of your journey, no matter how small. Whether you overcome your first pond maintenance challenge or enjoy a peaceful evening by the water, every moment is worth recognising.

Your pond is a testament to your creativity, dedication and connection to nature and deserves to be celebrated daily.

Inspiring the Next Wave

By sharing your story with others, you're not just participating in a community but inspiring the next wave of pond enthusiasts. Every photo, question or tip you share encourages someone else to take their first step into this fulfilling lifestyle.

Welcome to a world where every ripple tells a story, and every moment brings joy. Your pond is just the beginning of something magical, and I can't wait to see the ripples it creates in your garden, life and community.

Your pond story is just beginning, and I can't wait to see where it takes you. Building a pond is about more than creating a water feature – it transforms your garden, enriches your life and connects you with nature in ways you never imagined.

Here are a few ways to overcome intimidation:

- Go with your setup. A simple frog or patio pond can bring joy.
- Focus on what feels meaningful to you rather than on perfection or trends.
- View imperfections as part of the learning process.
- Use setbacks (like algae or maintenance struggles) as opportunities to grow.
- Celebrate every milestone, from adding your first plant to seeing your first lily bloom.

Here's how you can keep the ripples going:

Explore the possibilities. Dream big and try new things! Introduce plants that attract vibrant wildlife, expand your pond, or add features like a stream or waterfall. Each addition brings new joy and discovery.

Evolve gradually. Begin with essential features and add streams, waterfalls, or lighting over time. Experiment with different plants and fish to see what works best.

Pass it on. Share the pond lifestyle with others. Encourage friends, neighbours, or your children to create their water garden. Your enthusiasm might inspire them to take their first steps into this fulfilling hobby.

Share your journey. Join https://waterfeature.shop/community and connect with others who share your passion. Post photos, share stories and celebrate your milestones with a supportive community.

Your pond is more than just a feature in your garden – it's a gift to yourself, your loved ones and the planet. It's a sanctuary for wildlife, a retreat for relaxation and a space for creativity and connection.

Welcome to the pond lifestyle, where every ripple tells a story, and every moment brings joy.

Conclusion

As you reflect on your pond-building journey, take pride in your accomplishments. Whether your pond is large or small, it's a testament to your creativity, effort and passion. Following this book's guidance and choosing reliable, thoughtfully designed materials, you've built a thriving pond and an ecosystem. Your choice to prioritise durability and functionality has ensured a space that will stand the test of time, offering tranquillity and inspiration. Remember, every ripple in your pond is a reminder of your achievement.

Embrace the imperfections and challenges you've overcome. They've shaped your pond and your skills. As you enjoy the beauty and balance of your pond, know that you've taken a step toward a more rewarding and connected relationship with nature that begins with the slightest ripple and grows into a lasting legacy in your garden.

As we conclude this book, let's revisit the essential insights and powerful concepts highlighted throughout the chapters. Our journey began with exploring how ponds can enhance your garden and enrich your life. From selecting the ideal location and design to understanding the appropriate materials and techniques, you have the tools to create a pond that embodies your vision and suits your lifestyle.

Key Lessons Revisited

- You have acquired practical planning skills by considering space, purpose and available resources.
- You've had a chance to dive into the fun world of pond building, which includes excavation, lining and filtration.
- We dived into fostering ecosystems, selecting plants and ensuring your pond thrives year-round.
- Maintenance tips were shared to keep your pond clear and healthy without feeling overwhelming.
- Finally, stories of real pond owners like Kate and Gary illustrated that anyone can achieve a beautiful, serene pond with the proper guidance.

The underlying theme has been simple: You stop being a beginner when you build self-trust. Every step you've taken – digging, planting, adjusting – has built your confidence and brought you closer to mastering this rewarding craft. This book has equipped you with the tools to overcome challenges, embrace creativity, and enjoy the process of pond creation.

Your pond is more than just a feature in your garden. It's a reflection of your creativity, persistence and passion. Whether you've built a serene frog pond, a vibrant fish pond or an elegant water garden, your pond is a testament to your ability to transform an idea into reality.

It's easy to get caught up in striving for perfection but remember: Imperfection is perfection. A stray pebble, a misaligned plant or an unexpected visitor to your pond – all these quirks make it uniquely yours. Every ripple in the water reminds you of what you've accomplished, how far you've come and the joy you've brought to your space.

Your pond contributes to the environment on a broader level. It supports wildlife, promotes biodiversity and offers a serene retreat for you and your loved ones. The time, energy and care you've invested will create ripples beyond your garden, inspiring others and fostering a deeper connection with nature.

Continuing Your Pond Journey

Your pond-building journey doesn't have to stop here. There are countless ways to build on what you've learned and expand your connection to water features. Whether you're a beginner, enthusiast or professional, there's always more to explore, create and enjoy.

Explore pond kits. Planning your first pond or upgrading your current one? Visit https://waterfeature.shop/

beginner-pond-kits to explore our range of beginner-friendly pond kits and start your journey toward creating a stunning water feature with ease. Our professionally curated pond kits are tailored to your needs, helping you save time, avoid common mistakes, and achieve beautiful results effortlessly.

Join our POND community. Connect with like-minded pond enthusiasts through https://waterfeature.shop/community. This subscription-based hub offers exclusive resources, expert advice, and opportunities to share your journey with others who are passionate about water features.

Stay inspired. Follow my YouTube channel for worldwide pond-building tutorials, maintenance tips and inspiring success stories. Dive deeper by engaging with our vibrant social media groups to showcase your work, ask questions, and gain fresh ideas from a growing community of pond lovers.

Your Pond Journey Continues...

- Learn at Your Own Pace with POND School. Whether you're brand new to ponds, POND school offers beginner-friendly resources and tutorials to help you take your first steps with ease and confidence.

- Visit us at POND College in the heart of Northamptonshire, UK, for meet and greets, hands-on training, immersive practical workshops and live demonstrations. Whether you want to deepen your skills or gain confidence, our courses and events are designed to empower every level of pond builder or aquatic artist.

Explore all these opportunities here: https://waterfeature.shop/pond-perfection-for-beginners.

Take the next step. Reflect on your learning and set a goal for your next project – whether it's building your first pond, adding new plants, upgrading your filtration system, or even planning your next pond. Enjoy the process, knowing that every action brings you closer to your vision.

If there's one thing I want you to remember, it's this: Everything begins with a ripple. Don't wait for perfection; start with what you have. If your budget doesn't stretch to a pond kit right now, that's okay. What matters is that you take action and enjoy the water in your garden. After all, at its core, a pond is simply a hole filled with water—the challenge is keeping it clean and thriving. If you need help, I'm here for you.

Creating a pond is as much about the journey as the destination. It's about experimenting, learning from mistakes, and celebrating progress. Your pond is more than water and stones; it's a living piece of art that reflects your creativity and resilience.

Take a moment to look at your pond—or picture it. What do you see? A peaceful retreat, a hub of wildlife, or a statement of beauty? Whatever it is, it's uniquely yours, shaped by your vision and effort.

As you continue, remember that perfection isn't the goal. What makes your pond truly extraordinary is the journey of creating, learning, and growing.

Dream, plan and enjoy. This book was written to help you take action, build confidence, and share your passion. Whether you've already started or are still planning, don't wait—your perfect pond starts with the first step.

Take a moment to listen to the water, whether in your garden or in your imagination. Let it remind you of your accomplishments, and share your stories and experiences to inspire others.

Thank you for allowing me to guide you on this journey. I've loved writing this book, and I hope your pond brings you endless joy, serenity, and inspiration.

Mark 'The Pond Advisor'

www.ingramcontent.com/pod-product-compliance
Lightning Source LLC
Chambersburg PA
CBHW072012030526
44119CB00064B/608